LADO ENGLISH SERIES

by
ROBERT LADO

Dean, School of Languages and Linguistics
Georgetown University

with the collaboration of
ROGER TREMBLAY

Faculty of Arts
University of Sherbrooke

 **CEC** Centre Educatif et Culturel Inc.

8101, BOUL. MÉTROPOLITAIN, MONTRÉAL, QUÉ., H1J 1J9, TÉL. (514) 351-6010

ACKNOWLEDGEMENTS

The authors wish to express their sincerest thanks to those teachers and consultants, too numerous to mention, who gave so graciously of their time to present oral and written evaluations of the original edition and who contributed many useful suggestions for improvement.

*Illustrations by Bill Kresse, André Lemieux
and "Les Productions Klein Inc."*

PREFACE

The second edition of the *Lado English Series* contains six carefully graded levels, each of which includes a textbook, a workbook, and a teacher's manual. The audio-visual component consists of slides or filmstrips and tapes or cassettes. The central objective is to help the students learn to understand, speak, read, and write English for communication.

The chief innovative feature is CONTEXTUALIZATION—the presentation and practice of meaningful sentences in context, maintaining the advantages of grading and structurally focused learning. The new CONVERSATIONS are introduced by appropriate situations to provide a natural communicative setting. The former substitute sections are now contextualized as ADAPTATIONS which relate parts of the CONVERSATIONS to other realistic situations. Many contemporary illustrations have been included in the CONVERSATION, ADAPTATION, and PRACTICE sections to clarify meaning, add interest, and to serve as nonverbal cues. The New Edition has greater variety in the exercises and stresses active use of the language in activities that approximate full linguistic performance, for example, communication games and active listening.

The second edition has maintained simplicity of presentation in the following ways:

1) Each unit of the student's text is divided into sections with clear single-word headings to indicate the purpose of the sections: CONVERSATION, ADAPTATION, STUDY, PRACTICE, SPEAK, READ, THINK, PRONOUNCE.

2) In the first three books, each CONVERSATION section presents a dialogue which introduces the new material of the unit. These dialogues are shorter, easier to memorize, and contextualized through the use of illustrations.

3) The intonation accompanying each Conversation is one of many possibilities; however, the one chosen represents the most normal and natural pattern of a native English speaker. The intonation lines have been revised with curves substituted for the sharp corners. These lines represent the four intonation levels of English: low, mid, high, and extra high. The dot on the line indicates the principal stress in each sentence.

4) The ADAPTATION section takes parts of the CONVERSATION—usually a question and answer or a statement and comment—and provides cues to form similar mini-dialogues.

5) The STUDY sections present grammatical points in simple easy-to-read frames. In addition to examples, the STUDY frames include recommendations or rules for using the grammar points.

6) A PRACTICE section follows each STUDY to allow students to use correct English in speaking and writing. My experience has shown that students master the grammar best when they use it *at the same time* that they learn it in sentences. You will notice the advantages of pictures as visual cues in these sections.

Contextualization has resulted in a major reworking of the PRACTICE exercises. They are usually made up of pairs of sentences—question and answer, statement and comment—that make contextual sense while they exemplify the rule or feature of the frame. In many instances the responses are cued by pictures.

7) The SPEAK sections focus on using the newly learned vocabulary and grammar in new situations. The dialogues are not to be memorized; they are to be read aloud as in role-playing and then gradually changed by the students to express real information about themselves.

8) The READ sections aim to reinforce through silent reading what the students practiced and learned in earlier sections of the unit. Reading as a skill is developed gradually from a position subordinate to speaking in Book 1 to a position of major importance in Books 4, 5 and 6.

9) The THINK sections begin in Book 2. They provide the opportunity for freer and more creative use of English with the focus on thought as the starting point in the natural use of language. The pictures in these sections should inspire students to use newly acquired vocabulary and structures creatively.

10) The PRONOUNCE sections deal with those units of phonology which sometimes present problems in both understanding spoken English and speaking it. The PRONOUNCE sections progressively treat all of the phonemes of English, consonant clusters, stress, intonation, and particular trouble spots due to spelling. A facial diagram shows the formation of each sound.

Beginning with Book 2, the Series introduces a REFRESHER UNIT with corresponding INVENTORY tests to review the main grammatical points of the preceding book.

The six WORKBOOKS are designed to complement the learning activities covered in the six student texts. They offer additional exercises to master the points of each unit in *listening, reading,* and *writing*.

The six TEACHER'S MANUALS of the New Edition (one for each student text) have been considerably revised and expanded. The teaching suggestions for each unit list all of the new vocabulary and offer recommendations on how to teach each section. Games are occasionally suggested for variation from more formal learning techniques. There are also detailed notes on teaching the pronunciation features of each unit.

I am sure you will find this second edition of the *Lado English Series* both appealing and highly functional in teaching your students to use English for communication.

ROBERT LADO

Washington, D.C.

Foreword

This New Edition of the *Lado English Series* incorporates the results of a revision more extensive in scope than language teaching methods of proven efficacy habitually undergo. The changes introduced in this series are considerable and are the result of an evaluation of several years of use in a variety of Canadian contexts. This evaluation was conducted in two ways: informally, through personal contacts with hundreds of Quebec teachers within the context of *journées pédagogiques,* and systematically, through a questionnaire specifically designed for this purpose and completed by a cross section of teachers and consultants from the Province of Quebec.

The object of this evaluative research was not to completely rewrite the method, but to pinpoint those areas where the existing materials could be made to reflect more faithfully the needs of Canadian teachers and students. The information gathered helped to produce what twe feel are the very best materials for the Canadian context— materials which have been tried and tested in the milieu and which have been improved from comments and suggestions made by Canadian teachers. Never before, perhaps, have materials broadly international in character and appeal been so carefully tailored to the needs of a specific group of students. This New Edition is accordingly something of a landmark in Canadian publishing history and undeniably attests to the constantly increasing quality of E.S.L. teaching in this country.

Most of the changes in the series are of a pedagogic nature and concern both the presentation of the materials and the teaching strategies. Much effort has been expended on introducing activities which enable the student to use the language in a variety of meaningful situations, thus downplaying the purely mechanical drills at the heart of most textbooks. For pedagogical reasons and also in response to requests from the users of the first edition, we have introduced some important changes in the sequencing and presentation of certain linguistic structures, such as presenting the present progressive tense in Book 1 rather than in Book 2.

Some exciting new features have been added to the New Edition. For example, we have prepared a teacher's manual and testing materials for each of the six levels. The teacher's manuals present some explicit and varied instructions for class management together with many useful suggestions for games and other complementary activities. The slides have been redone to make them easier to use and more interesting and appealing. The exercises involve a greater variety of learning situations such as independent work activities, paired activities, and small group or whole class activites.

All the changes incorporated in the new *Lado English Series* are intended to better suit your needs as well as those of your students. We have no doubt that you will find the materials both interesting and easy to use, and that they will help you to lead your students toward greater proficiency in English.

ROGER TREMBLAY

Faculty of Arts
University of Sherbrooke
Sherbrooke, Quebec

TABLE OF CONTENTS

UNIT 1

Discussing a recent event.

John:

Where were you last night?

Paul:

I was at the fair with Alice.

John:

The fair! When did it begin?

Paul:

It began yesterday.

John:

How was it?

Paul:

It was terrific. We loved it.

John:

What did you see?

Paul:

We saw animals and the pie-eating contest.

ADAPTATION

Construct new sentences like the models using the cues.

 1

you, last night?
I, fair.

Where were you last night?
I was at the fair.

they, yesterday?

they, museum.

_____ ?

_____ .

Paul, this morning?

he, post office.

_____ ?

_____ .

she, last Sunday?

she, theater.

_____ ?

_____ .

3

2

the fair, begin?
yesterday.

When did the fair begin?
It began yesterday.

the circus, end?

last night.

_____ ?

_____ .

the store, close?

at eight o'clock.

_____ ?

_____ .

school, start?

yesterday.

_____ ?

_____ .

3

it?
terrific.

How was it?
It was terrific. We loved it.

the pie-eating contest?

funny.

_____ ?

_____ . _____ .

4

the food?   _____ ?

delicious.   _____ . _____ .

the bingo game?   _____ ?

interesting.   _____ . _____ .

you see?
the pie-eating contest.

What did you see?
We saw the pie-eating contest.

Alice like?   _____ ?

the ferris wheel.   _____ .

she eat?   _____ ?

a hamburger.   _____ .

they drink?   _____ ?

soda.   _____ .

Information questions in the past: *What did you see?*

Notice the position of the question words WHAT, WHO(M), WHERE, WHEN, HOW:

| | DID you see the game? | No, we didn't. |
| WHAT | DID you see? | |

| | DID you see John? | No, we didn't. |
| WHO(M) | DID you see? | |

| | DID you go to the city? | No, we didn't. |
| WHERE | DID you go? | |

| | DID it begin at six? | No, it didn't. |
| WHEN | DID it begin? | |

| | DID it begin with music? | No, it didn't. |
| HOW | DID it begin? | |

Use the appropriate question word (WHAT, WHO(M), WHERE, WHEN, HOW) at the beginning of a question.

1 Ask and answer questions using the pictures as cues.

Did you go *to the city*?

No, I didn't.

Where did you go?

I went to the circus.

Did she see *the circus*?

No, she didn't.

What did she see?

She saw a play.

Did it begin *at five*?

_____ .

_____ ?

_____ .

Did they eat *at a restaurant*?

_____ .

_____ ?

_____ .

7

Did they read *the newspaper*?

_____ .

_____ ?

_____ .

Did she see *Paul*?

_____ .

_____ ?

_____ .

Did he go *by car*?

_____ .

_____ ?

_____ .

Bill

2 Ask the appropriate information question based on the statement.

I went to the circus, but she didn't.

→ **Where did she go?**

John saw the city, but Bill didn't.

→ **What did he see?**

We arrived at five o'clock, but they didn't.

→ **When did they arrive?**

We ate at a restaurant, but they didn't.

I spoke English, but she didn't.

We went home at three-thirty, but you didn't.

We saw a TV program, but he didn't.

They went to the museum, but Vincent didn't.

Helen read the book, but Paul didn't.

I went by car, but he didn't.

We began yesterday, but they didn't.

STUDY 2

Information questions with BE in the past: *How was it?*

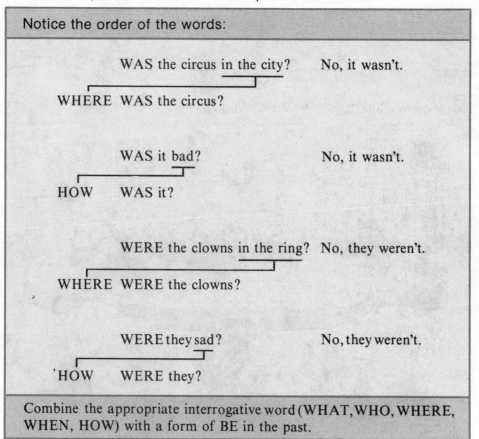

Notice the order of the words:

WAS the circus in the city?   No, it wasn't.

WHERE WAS the circus?

WAS it bad?   No, it wasn't.

HOW   WAS it?

WERE the clowns in the ring? No, they weren't.

WHERE WERE the clowns?

WERE they sad?   No, they weren't.

'HOW   WERE they?

Combine the appropriate interrogative word (WHAT, WHO, WHERE, WHEN, HOW) with a form of BE in the past.

1 Give the information questions using *what, who, where, when, how*.

When was the circus?   **The circus was** *yesterday*.
Where were the lions?   **The lions were** *in the ring*.

_____ ? The clown was *funny*.

_____ ? His name was *Bozo*.

_____ ? *Paul* was there.

_____ ? The children were *happy*.

_____ ? Susan and Vincent were *home*.

_____ ? They were *sick*.

2 Answer the questions according to the picture.

Where did Paul go?

→ **He went to the circus.**

Who did he see?

→ **He saw John and Helen.**

When did the show begin?

What did they see, acrobats or paintings?

How were the clowns, funny or dull?

What did Paul eat, peanuts or popcorn?

Where was the lion?

How were the acrobats, excellent or bad?

Where was the trainer, in the cage or in the ring?

Where were the horses?

SPEAK

1 Alice and Paul

A.: Good morning, Paul. How are you?

P.: Fine, thanks. How's David?

A.: He's fine today, but he was sick yesterday.

P.: Yes, I know. He didn't play tennis yesterday.

A.: Did you play tennis?

P.: Yes, I did. I played with Ann.

A.: Where did you play?

P.: We played at MacDonald Park.

A.: How was the game?

P.: It was terrific. I won.

2 Prepare a dialogue between a policeman and an eye-witness to an automobile accident. Use the following information.

I saw an accident on Main Street. It was ten o'clock. It was dark. A car hit a little girl. The little girl was in the street. The little girl fell. The little girl was hurt. She was afraid. The car stopped. I called the police.

Policeman: **Where did you see the accident?**

Witness: **I saw...**

Continue the dialogue.

READ

Last June Gloria and Pat went on vacation to California. Every evening Gloria wrote about her activities in her diary. On Monday Gloria wrote:

Dear Diary,

Today we visited San Francisco. Pat and I liked the city. In the morning we visited a beautiful church and an old monastery. In the center of town we saw a statue. It was a statue of Balboa. He discovered the Pacific Ocean in 1513.

In the evening we ate at a Mexican restaurant. The food was delicious. We had fun!

Answer the questions.

1. Where did Gloria and Pat go on vacation?

2. When did they go?

3. Where did Gloria describe her activities?

4. What did they visit in the morning?

5. What did they see in the center of town?

6. What did Balboa discover?

7. When did he discover it?

8. Where did Gloria and Pat eat?

9. How was the food?

Discover the meanings of IN and ON by looking at the pictures.

The water is IN the pitcher.

The pitcher is ON the table.

Construct sentences like the models. Use the pictures as cues.

frog / bottle

→ **The frog is in the bottle.**

book / table

→ **The book is on the table.**

picture / wall

woman / kitchen

fish / water

THINK

The clown put his flower in the vase, but the vase was on a very tall stand. How did he put the flower in the vase?

(Use *First, then, put ... on ..., got up, put ..., in ..., fell down*.)

First, he put the box on the trunk. Then, he put the chair on ...

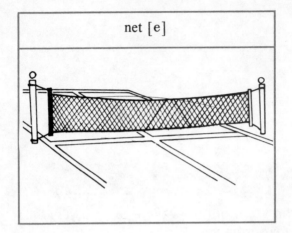

net [e]

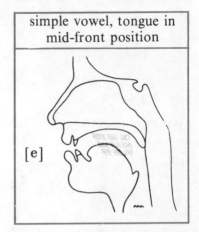

simple vowel, tongue in mid-front position

[e]

net	get	friend	address
pen	bed	Helen	elephant
tell	then	French	excellent
bread	tent	when	expensive
desk	cents	went	restaurant

My friends and I went to the circus yesterday.

Did Helen like the elephants?

Yes, she did. Wendy counted ten of them in the tent.

16

How was the French restaurant?

It was excellent, but it was expensive.

When did you go?

We went last Wednesday.

What's the address?

Eleven-seventy Kent Street.

UNIT 2

Talking about last weekend.

Nathan:

What did you do last Saturday?

Michael:

I rode my motorcycle. What did you do?

Nathan:

I went to the library.

Michael:

The library! What did you do there?

Nathan:

I read a book on transportation.

Michael:

Did you read all day?

Nathan:

No. I did my homework in the afternoon.

ADAPTATION

Construct new sentences like the models using the cues.

you, Saturday?
rode my motorcycle.

What did you do last Saturday?
I rode my motorcycle.

she, month?

_____ ?

went to Jamaica.

_____ .

he, weekend?

_____ ?

went to the fair.

_____ .

they, night?

_____ ?

played the guitar.

_____ .

19

2

you?
went to the library.

What did you do?
I went to the library.

she?

_____ ?

wrote a letter.

_____ .

he?

_____ ?

read a story.

_____ .

Jane?

_____ ?

saw a play.

_____ .

3

you, there?
read a book.

What did you do there?
I read a book.

he, in Montreal?

_____ ?

went to a museum.

_____ .

20

they, in Quebec?

_____ ?

learned French.

_____ .

she, in school?

_____ ?

played basketball.

_____ .

4

you, read?
did my homework.

Did you read all day?
No. I did my homework in the afternoon.

she, play?

_____ ?

visited John.

___._____ .

they, read?

_____ ?

went to a movie.

___._____ .

he, work?

_____ ?

slept.

___._____ .

Information questions about the verb phrase: *What did you do last weekend?*

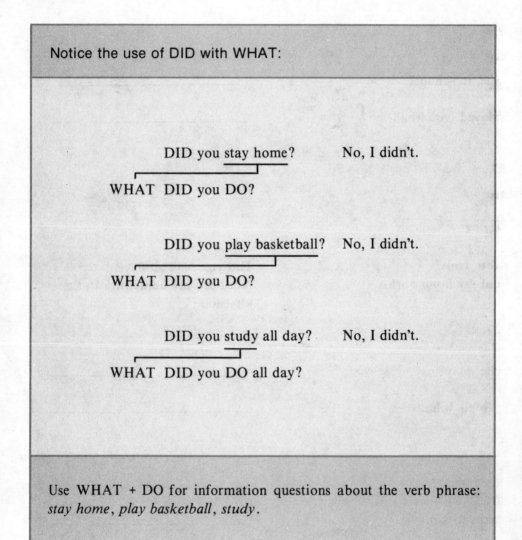

Notice the use of DID with WHAT:

DID you stay home?	No, I didn't.
WHAT DID you DO?	
DID you play basketball?	No, I didn't.
WHAT DID you DO?	
DID you study all day?	No, I didn't.
WHAT DID you DO all day?	

Use WHAT + DO for information questions about the verb phrase: *stay home, play basketball, study.*

1 Construct mini-dialogues using the pictures as cues.

Did you play basketball last weekend?

No, I didn't.

What did you do?

I played the guitar.

Did Bill stay home on Sunday?

No, he didn't.

What did he do?

He went to the theater.

Did John play soccer yesterday?

_____ .

_____ ?

_____ .

Did Alice go to bed early last night?

_____ .

_____ ?

_____ .

Did they study all day?

_____ .

_____ ?

_____ .

Did you go to the movies last
Friday?

_____ .

_____ ?

_____ .

Did you stay home last week?

_____ .

_____ ?

_____ .

Did Susan practice the piano?

_____ .

_____ ?

_____ .

2 Answer the questions according to the pictures.

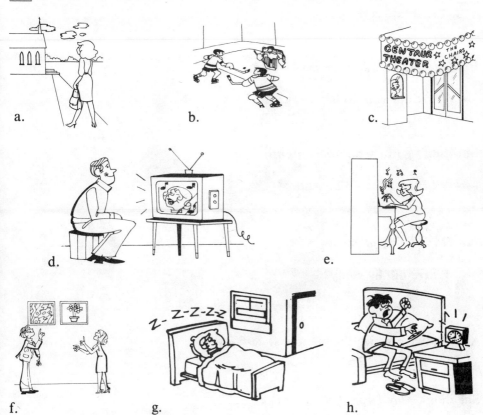

a.

b.

c.

d.

e.

f.

g.

h.

a. **What did you do last Sunday, stay home or go to church?**
   → **I went to church.**

b. **What did Bill do, play hockey with friends or study?**
   → **He played hockey with friends.**

c. What did Alice do yesterday, go to the theater or stay home?

d. What did Bill do, study geography or watch television?

e. What did Alice do last night, play the piano or visit Nancy?

f. What did they do last Monday, go to the museum or study geography?

g. What did you do last night, practice the piano or go to bed early?

h. What did you do in the morning, get up early or sleep late?

3 Ask an information question about the phrase in italics. Follow the examples.

I didn't *play basketball* last weekend.

→ **What did you do last weekend?**

She didn't go to school *last month*.

→ **When did she go to school?**

Bill didn't study *at home*.

→ **Where did he study?**

Alice didn't practice the piano *last Sunday*.

She didn't *play basketball* last week.

I didn't study history *in school*.

They didn't *watch television* last night.

The clown didn't put the flower *in the vase*.

John didn't go to school *on Monday*.

He didn't *see the circus* last weekend.

Short answers to information questions: *Last summer*.

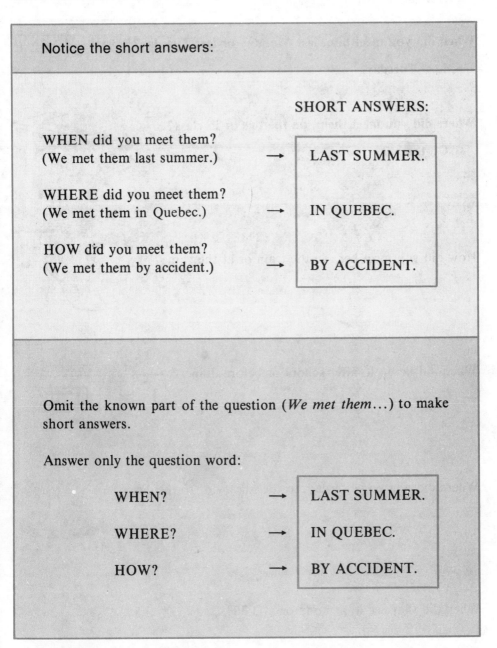

Notice the short answers:

SHORT ANSWERS:

WHEN did you meet them?
(We met them last summer.) → LAST SUMMER.

WHERE did you meet them?
(We met them in Quebec.) → IN QUEBEC.

HOW did you meet them?
(We met them by accident.) → BY ACCIDENT.

Omit the known part of the question (*We met them...*) to make short answers.

Answer only the question word:

WHEN? → LAST SUMMER.

WHERE? → IN QUEBEC.

HOW? → BY ACCIDENT.

1 Answer the questions according to the pictures. Use short answers.

When did you meet him, last Monday or last Tuesday?

→ **Last Tuesday.**

Where did you meet them, on the bus or in class?

→ **On the bus.**

How did you meet her, on the train or at the game?

When did he do it, after school or before dinner?

Where did you go yesterday, to the library or to the circus?

When did they see it, at noon or at 3:30?

Where did she get it, in Hawaii or in Japan?

Where did you talk to her,
at the post office or at the store?

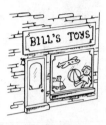

2 Answer the questions according to the pictures. Use short answers.

a. **How did he go to the airport?**
   → **By taxi** .

b. **Where did he go?**

c. **Where did he meet his friend?**

d. **Where did they eat lunch?**

29

e. Where did they work?

f. How did he go to the airport?

g. When did he arrive home?

STUDY 3

Months of the year: *January, February*...

Learn the twelve months of the year:

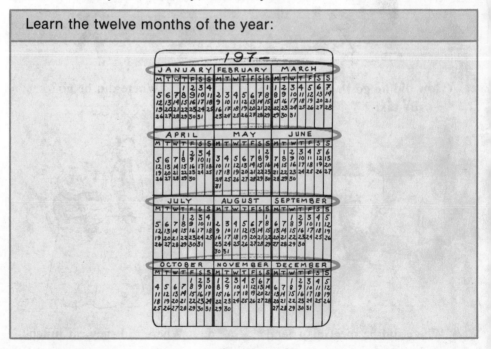

Thirty days have September,
April, June, and November;
February has twenty-eight.
All the rest have thirty-one,
Except in leap year
When February has twenty-nine.

PRACTICE

1 Say the months of the year.

2 Say: "Thirty days have September,…"

3 Answer the questions individually.

What months have 30 days?

What months have 31 days?

What month has 28 days?

When does February have 29 days?

SPEAK

1 Charles and David

C.: Do you know Mary?

D.: Yes, I do.

C.: When did you meet her?

D.: Last August.

C.: Where were you last August?

D.: In Maine.

C.: How did you meet her?

D.: Sylvia introduced us.

2 Helen and Paul

H.: What did you do last Sunday?

P.: I read the paper and went to church.

H.: Did you go out with your friends too?

P.: No, I stayed home. What did you do?

H.: I went to church in the morning. In the afternoon I studied.

READ

A year in Canada has four seasons: spring, summer, fall and winter. Spring has three months: March, April and May. In March the weather is cold, but the snow melts. It's maple syrup time. In spring the weather is nice; the trees are green, and people are happy.

Summer is the season after spring. The summer months are June, July and August. In summer the weather is hot. School ends and vacations begin. People go to the beach and they go on picnics. Summer is short.

Fall is the season after summer. The fall months are September, October and November. The weather is nice in September, but school begins. The weekends are fun. In October the leaves change color and fall from the trees.

Winter is the season after fall. December is cold, but Christmas is fun. In January and February snow falls. Children play in the snow, and people ski and skate. But winter is long.

Answer the questions.

1. What are the four seasons in Canada?

2. What is the weather in March?

3. What comes after spring?

4. What do people do in the summer?

5. When does school begin?

6. When does it snow?

7. What do people do in the winter?

8. Is winter long in Canada?

What did he (she) do each month?

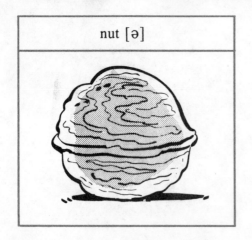

PRONOUNCE

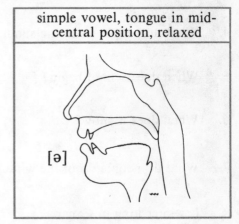

nut [ə]

simple vowel, tongue in mid-central position, relaxed

[ə]

nut	month	circus	mother
study	London	dull	young
cover	does	some	trunk
hungry	up	country	funny
ugly	lunch	doesn't	summer

Was the zoo interesting? Yes!

The monkeys were funny and hungry.

Mother gave them some nuts for lunch.

Is the book dull?

No, it's not.

Well, the cover is ugly.

Don't judge a book by its cover.

UNIT 3

Seeing a friend at an unexpected place.

Henry:

What were you doing at the courthouse yesterday?

Joan:

I was waiting for my uncle.

Henry:

What was he doing there?

Joan:

He was working. He's a lawyer. Were you there too?

Henry:

Yes, I was.

Joan:

What were you doing there?

36

Henry:

I was getting a driver's license.

ADAPTATION

Construct new sentences like the models using the cues.

you, courthouse?

What were you doing at the courthouse yesterday?

waiting for my uncle.

I was waiting for my uncle.

he, post office?

_____ ?

buying stamps.

_____ .

they, music store?

_____ ?

looking at records.

_____ .

she, bus station?

_____ ?

waiting for me.

_____ .

you, library?

_____ ?

reading a magazine.

_____ .

2

he, there?

working. lawyer.

What was he doing there?

He was working. He's a lawyer.

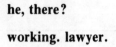

Paul, at the library?

studying. student.

_____ ?

_____ . _____ .

the women, there?

selling books. saleswomen.

_____ ?

_____ . _____ .

the men, on the boat?

fishing. fishermen.

_____ ?

_____ . _____ .

she, at the airport.

working. stewardess.

_____ ?

_____ . _____ .

38

3

you, there?	Were you there too?
Yes.	**Yes, I was.**

she, at home? 　　　　　　　　　＿＿＿＿＿＿＿＿＿＿＿＿ ?

No. 　　　　　　　　　　　　　＿＿＿＿＿＿＿＿＿＿＿＿ .

they, in Ottawa? 　　　　　　　＿＿＿＿＿＿＿＿＿＿＿＿ ?

Yes. 　　　　　　　　　　　　　＿＿＿＿＿＿＿＿＿＿＿＿ .

he, at the post office? 　　　　＿＿＿＿＿＿＿＿＿＿＿＿ ?

Yes. 　　　　　　　　　　　　　＿＿＿＿＿＿＿＿＿＿＿＿ .

they, in the living room? 　　　＿＿＿＿＿＿＿＿＿＿＿＿ ?

No. 　　　　　　　　　　　　　＿＿＿＿＿＿＿＿＿＿＿＿ .

you, here? 　　　　　　　　　　＿＿＿＿＿＿＿＿＿＿＿＿ ?

Yes. 　　　　　　　　　　　　　＿＿＿＿＿＿＿＿＿＿＿＿ .

4

you, there?	What were you doing there?
getting a driver's license.	**I was getting a driver's license.**

the girls, in the park? 　　　　＿＿＿＿＿＿＿＿＿＿＿＿ ?

playing baseball. 　　　　　　　＿＿＿＿＿＿＿＿＿＿＿＿ .

39

they, in Vancouver? _____ ?

visiting Peter. _____ .

he, at the office? _____ ?

working. _____ .

STUDY 1

Past progressive form: *I was waiting*.

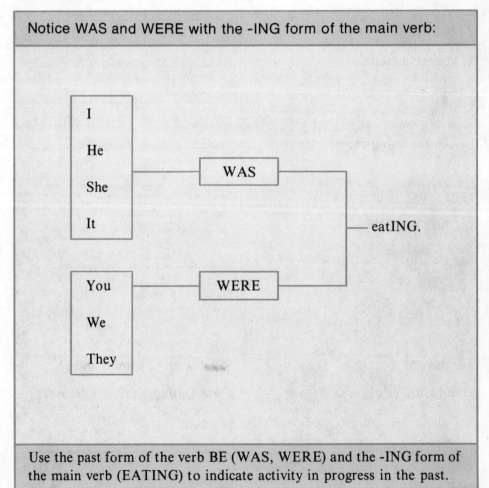

Notice WAS and WERE with the -ING form of the main verb:

I He She It	WAS	
		eatING.
You We They	WERE	

Use the past form of the verb BE (WAS, WERE) and the -ING form of the main verb (EATING) to indicate activity in progress in the past.

40

CONTRAST

> I ate lunch.
>
> I was eating lunch.

I ate: activity completed in the past.

I was eating: activity in progress in the past.

PRACTICE

1 Change the verbs to the past progressive form. Use the pictures to complete the statements.

Helen / visit

→ **Helen was visiting Paul.**

Paul

You / go home

→ **You were going home at five o'clock.**

I / read

Henry / write

41

My brother / study

Bill / work

Nancy / sing

2 What was the family doing at seven o'clock?

Negative past progressive form: *I wasn't waiting*.

Notice WASN'T and WEREN'T with the -ING form of the main verb:

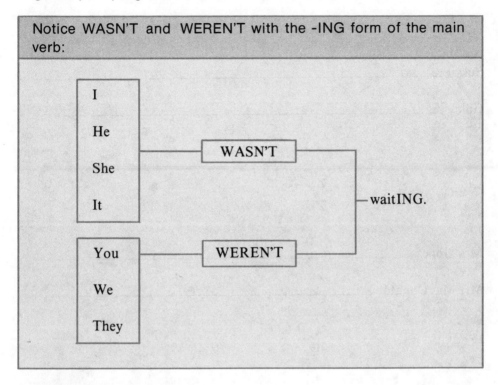

Make two statements about each picture using the affirmative and the negative. Follow the example.

Paul was eating but Mary wasn't eating.
Mary was reading but Paul wasn't reading.

He _____ .

She _____ .

Susan _____ .

Gilles _____ .

Mrs. Jones _____ .

Mr. MacDonald _____ .

Mr. Bunker _____ .

Mrs. Bunker _____ .

Mr. Spicer _____ .

Mrs. Spicer _____ .

Past progressive interrogative form: *Wasn't I waiting?*

Notice the order of the words:

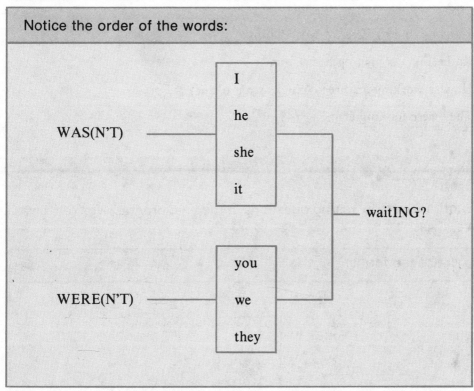

Change to yes/no questions using the new object or verb and *too*.

Bill was helping Alice. / Gloria?
→ **Was he helping Gloria too?**

I was waiting for my sister. / brother?
→ **Were you waiting for your brother too?**

He was listening to music. / the news?
→ **Was he listening to the news too?**

They were reading the paper. / a book?

We were visiting her. / him?

Nancy was resting. / reading?

They were dancing. / singing?

I was talking to Peter. / Mr. Philips?

Katherine was visiting her. / him?

He was working at three o'clock. / ten o'clock?

They were looking at me. / us?

Short answers to yes/no questions in the past progressive: *Yes, I was. No, I wasn't.*

Notice the forms:

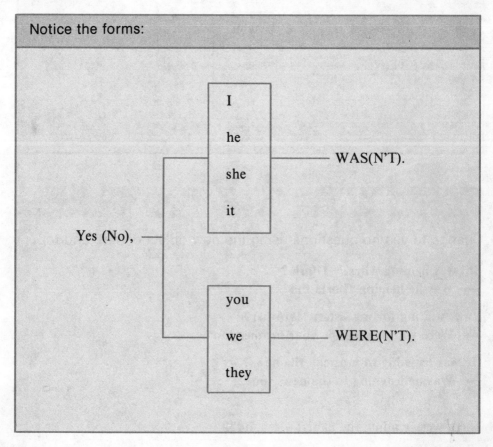

Yes (No),

I
he
she
it
— WAS(N'T).

you
we
they
— WERE(N'T).

Answer according to the pictures. Use short answers.

Was he sleeping?

→ **Yes, he was.**

Was Bill giving coffee to Helen?

→ **No, he wasn't.**

Was John working at the hospital?

Were they visiting a museum?

Was he eating?

Was Philip reading the paper?

Was Susan playing the piano?

Were they playing baseball?

Information questions with the past progressive: *What was he doing*?

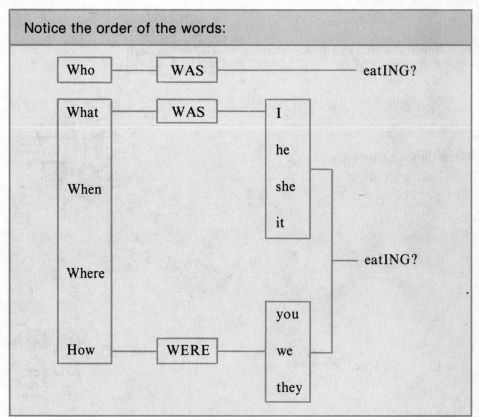

1 Create mini-dialogues like the models.

Was Mary working *at the hospital*?
No, she wasn't.
Where was she working?
At the post office.

Was Victor visiting *Nancy*?
No, he wasn't.
Who was he visiting?
Bill.

Bill

Were you *eating* **at the restaurant?**
No, I wasn't.
What were you doing at the restaurant?
Waiting for John.

John

Was Ann helping *Gloria*?

_____ .

_____ ?

Helen

_____ .

49

Was the singer *at home*?

_____ .

_____ ?

_____ .

Were you waiting there *in the morning*?

_____ .

_____ ?

_____ .

evening

Was Bill going *to Canada*?

_____ .

_____ ?

_____ .

ITALY

Were he and Helen going *by bus*?

_____ .

_____ ?

_____ .

Was he playing *basketball*?

_____ .

_____ ?

_____ .

2 Answer according to the pictures.

What was John doing at the restaurant, eating or working?
→ **He was working.**

Who was Vincent helping, Helen or Bill?
→ **He was helping Helen.**

Where was he waiting, in school or at home?
→ **He was waiting at home.**

What were you taking to him, flowers or coffee?

How was he going home, by bus or by taxi?

When was John writing a letter, last Tuesday or last night?

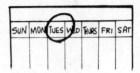

Who was Henry visiting, Jane or Alice?

Alice

What was he doing, thinking or talking?

Where were they going, to Quebec or to New York?

How were they going, by bus or by plane?

When were they going, at two o'clock or at three o'clock?

1 Benjamin and Janet

B.: What were you doing at the store yesterday?

J.: I was visiting Barbara.

B.: Was Barbara buying things for school?

J.: No, she wasn't. She was working. She's a saleswoman there.

53

2 Allen and John

A.: Hello, John. Were you visiting your sister at the hospital this morning?

J.: No, I wasn't. I was waiting for Bill.

A.: What was he doing there?

J.: He was taking some books to his father.

A.: Oh, is his father sick?

J.: No, he isn't. His father's a doctor. He works there.

3 Prepare a dialogue between Paul and Mary. Use the information in the following text.

Last Saturday Paul was at the bus station. He was going to Granby and he was waiting for the bus. He was reading. He wasn't reading a magazine. He was reading a history book. He was studying for an exam. Mary saw Paul at the bus station, but she did not talk to him.

Mary: **What were you doing at the bus station last Saturday?**
Paul: **I was...**

Continue the dialogue.

READ

John was reading a science magazine yesterday. He was reading about the discovery of penicillin.

"Doctor Alexander Fleming was studying bacteria in London in 1928. One day he was working in his office. He was looking at germs. Some of the germs were dying. Something was growing on them and killing them.

"Dr. Fleming remembered a little girl with these germs in her body. She was very sick. Then he thought about the germs in his office. Something was killing them. What was it? Dr. Fleming prepared some medicine and gave it to the girl. It made her well. He named it penicillin."

Answer the questions.

1. What was John reading?

2. What was Dr. Fleming doing in 1928?

3. Where was he studying bacteria?

4. What was growing on the germs?

5. What did the little girl have in her body?

6. What did Dr. Fleming give her?

THINK

What was Dr. Fleming doing?

Contrast [e] and [ə].

net [e]	nut [ə]
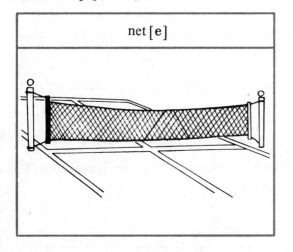	

desk	pencil	does	lunch
slept	excuse	come	judge
Dennis	address	club	subject
question	invent	cover	number
medicine	chemistry	trunk	discuss

My brother is an engineer. Last month he went to Toronto for ten days. He was studying a subway system there.

Who were the men at the bus station?
Engineers. They're building the new Prince Edward Hotel.

Yesterday Fred got a letter from his cousin in Colombia. She discussed Colombian sculpture.

UNIT 4

Getting help.

Child:

Are we going to walk home?

Mother:

No, we're not. We're going to get help.

Child:

Are you going to call Dad?

Mother:

No. I'm going to call a garage.

Child:

Is a mechanic going to come here?

Mother:

Yes, he is.

Child:

What is he going to do?

Mother:

He's going to tow the car.

ADAPTATION

Construct new sentences like the models using the cues.

walk home?	**Are we going to walk home?**
get help.	**No, we're not. We're going to get help.**

visit Alice?   _____ ?

write her a letter.   _____ . _____ .

see the play?   _____ ?

stay home.   _____ . _____ .

watch the game?   _____ ?

play tennis.   _____ . _____ .

help David?   _____ ?

study.   _____ . _____ .

59

2

you, call Dad?   **Are you going to call Dad?**

call a garage.   **No. I'm going to call a garage.**

he, sing a song?   _____ ?

play the piano.   _____ . _____ .

she, study English?   _____ ?

study French.   _____ . _____ .

John, fix the car?   _____ ?

eat lunch.   _____ . _____ .

Betty, walk?   _____ ?

take a taxi.   _____ . _____ .

3

a mechanic?   **Is a mechanic going to come?**

                                   Yes, he is.

a taxi?   _____ ?

                             _____ .

the doctor?

_____ ?

_____ .

a truck?

_____ ?

_____ .

the mailman?

_____ ?

_____ .

4

he?

tow the car.

What is he going to do?

He's going to tow the car.

she?

_____ ?

play tennis.

_____ .

Daniel?

_____ ?

watch the game.

_____ .

Ann? _____ ?

buy some clothes. _____ .

Martha? _____ ?

work late. _____ .

The future with GOING TO: *I'm going to call a garage.*

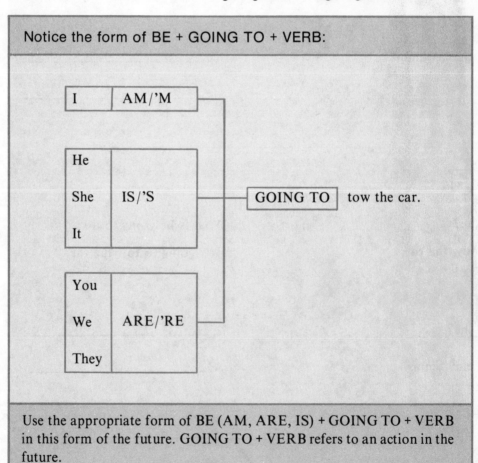

Notice the form of BE + GOING TO + VERB:

I	AM/'M		

He / She / It — IS/'S

GOING TO — tow the car.

You / We / They — ARE/'RE

Use the appropriate form of BE (AM, ARE, IS) + GOING TO + VERB in this form of the future. GOING TO + VERB refers to an action in the future.

62

1 Each person is GOING TO do something TOMORROW. What is it?

a. They

b. Bill and Mr. Smith

c. You

d. Ida

e. Robert

f. Alice

g. Mr. Collins

h. Mr. and Mrs. Coleman

i. Peter

j. You

a. **They're going to play tennis tommorow.**

b. **Bill and Mr. Smith are going to talk tomorrow.**

2 Construct an affirmative and a negative statement with *going to* for each picture.

Paul is going to study. He's not going to play tennis.

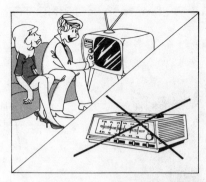

They're going to watch TV. They're not going to listen to the radio.

We're _____ .

_____ .

I'm _____ .

_____ .

They're _____ .

_____ .

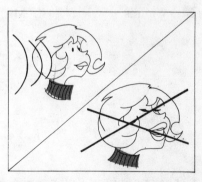

She's _____ .

_____ .

Interrogative statements with GOING TO: *Is a mechanic going to come?*

Notice the order of the words:

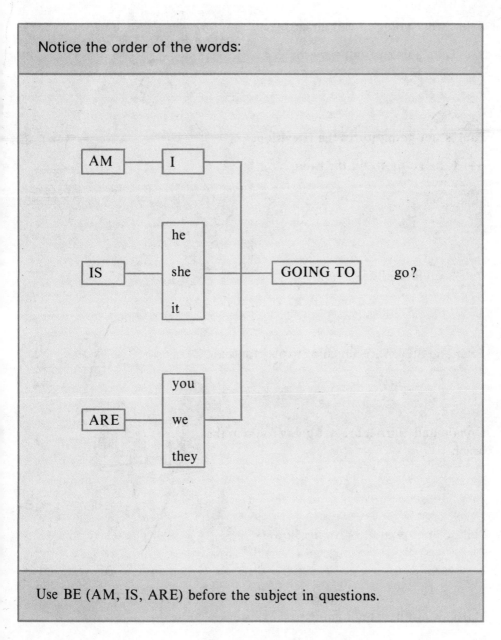

Use BE (AM, IS, ARE) before the subject in questions.

Construct questions based on the statements using the pictures as cues.

John is not going to call an engineer.

→ **Is he going to call a mechanic?**

Paul is not going to fix the television.

→ **Is he going to fix the radio?**

Marie is not going to study.

Peter and Steven are not going to play football.

Donald and Harriet are not going to go to the beach.

Philip is not going to give me flowers.

Martha's mother is not going to make a cake.

66

Short answers to yes/no questions with GOING TO: *Yes, he is.*
No, he's not.

Notice the short answer forms:

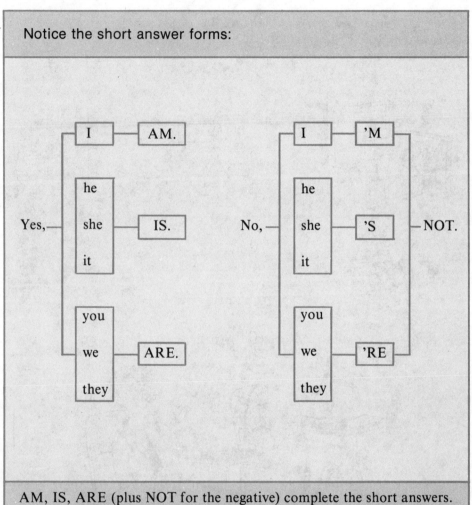

AM, IS, ARE (plus NOT for the negative) complete the short answers.
Use contractions for the negative form only. ISN'T, AREN'T are other
contractions of IS NOT, ARE NOT.

1 Answer according to the pictures. Use short answers.

a.

b.

c.

d.

e.

f.

g.

h.

Henry

Michael

a. Is Paul going to stay home?
→ No, he's not.

b. Are James and Paul going to play tennis?
→ Yes, they are.

c. Is James going to study astronomy?

d. Henry, are you going to go out Saturday?

e. Is James going to work at the restaurant?

f. Michael, is Helen going to go to the movies?

g. Are James and Paul going to see the dentist?

h. Is James going to read the geography books?

2 Change to yes/no questions using the cues. Then answer the questions according to the pictures.

John is going to study this evening. / Paul?
→ Is Paul going to study this evening?
→ No, he's not.

I'm going to go out. / they?
→ Are they going to go out?
→ Yes, they are.

He's going to play the guitar. / you?
→ Are you going to play the guitar?
→ Yes, I am.

We're going to use our notes. / you?

Helen is going to teach English. / Kenneth?

They're going to come to class tomorrow. / he?

I'm going to sing a song. / they?

Mrs. Fleming is going to write the answers. / Mr. Martin?

You're going to ask many questions. / Kenneth?

70

1 Karen and Jill

K.: Are you going to go out now?

J.: Yes. I'm going to play tennis with Thomas.

K.: Are Susan and Robert going to play too?

J.: No, they aren't. Susan is going to take pictures, and Robert is going to help her.

2 Michael, Anthony, and Joyce

M.: Hello, Anthony. Who's your new friend?
Aren't you going to introduce me?

A.: Sure. Michael, this is Joyce Hill.

M.: Hello, Joyce. Are you going to move into our neighborhood?

J.: I don't know yet.

71

3 Benjamin and Francis

B.: Is the rodeo going to begin at eight?

F.: Yes, it is, but I'm going to arrive early.

B.: Are you going to take Margaret with you?

F.: Yes. I'm going to take Margaret and Paul.
They love horses and cowboys.

READ

Donald and Peter are brothers. In the winter they like to ski in the Laurentians. They are planning a ski trip for this weekend, but they don't know about the weather. Tonight they are going to listen to the weather forecast on the radio.

At 7:30 the weatherman announces the weather for the weekend:

"Friday is going to be cold and cloudy. It's not going to rain. The temperature is going to be below zero. It's going to snow Friday night and maybe Saturday morning too. Saturday afternoon and Sunday are going to be clear, cold and sunny."

Now Donald and Peter are excited. The weather forecast is good. The weather is going to be perfect for a ski trip.

Answer the questions.

1. Are Donald and Peter going to ski or play tennis?

2. What are they planning?

3. Are they going to listen to the weather forecast on the radio or on TV?

4. Is the weather going to be rainy on Friday?

5. Where are Donald and Peter going to go this weekend?

6. Is it going to snow Friday night or Saturday afternoon?

7. What time was the weather forecast?

8. Is Sunday going to be cloudy or clear?

9. Do Donald and Peter like the forecast?

THINK

Ask each other questions about the pictures. Use *going to*.

PRONOUNCE

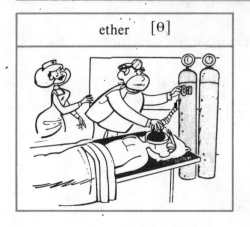

ether [θ]

friction between tongue upper teeth, voiceless

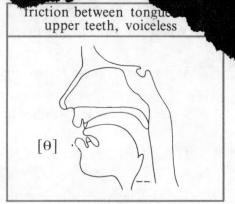

[θ]

74

three	think	thirsty	tooth
thirteen	Thursday	thirt...	...onth
theater	Kathleen	E...	...anks
Elizabeth	mathematics	...	...enneth

Kathleen's birthday is next Thursday.
She is going to be thirteen.

Are Elizabeth and Martha at home?
No, they aren't. They're studying math at Ethel's.

When did Kenneth go to the theater with h... ...ily?
Last month, I think.

UNIT 5

Planning to go to a game.

Dennis:

What are you going to do on Saturday?

Jason:

We're going to watch the hockey game.

Dennis:

Who is going to play?

Jason:

Toronto and Montreal.

Dennis:

Where are you going to buy tickets?

Jason:

At the Forum.

Dennis:

When does the ticket window open?

Jason:

An hour before the game.

ADAPTATION

Construct new sentences like the models using the cues.

1

you, on Saturday?

What are you going to do on Saturday?

watch the hockey game.

We're going to watch the hockey game.

she, tomorrow?

_____ ?

buy a hat.

_____ .

he, next week?

_____ ?

go to New York.

_____

they, on Tuesday?   _____ ?

play tennis.   _____ .

we, Monday?   _____ ?

see the play.   _____ .

2

play?   **Who is going to play?**

Toronto, Montreal.   **Toronto and Montreal.**

sing?   _____ ?

Peter, Mary.   _____ .

study?   _____ ?

You, I.   _____ .

write it?   _____ ?

Dennis, his friend.   _____ .

cook?   _____ ?

My sister, her son.   _____ .

78

buy tickets?

at, Forum.

Where are you going to buy tickets?

At the Forum.

sing the song?

at, club.

_____ ?

_____ .

write the exercises?

in, classroom.

_____ ?

_____ .

play tennis?

in, gymnasium.

_____ ?

_____ .

eat lunch?

in, cafeteria.

_____ ?

_____ .

Information questions in the future with GOING TO: *What are you going to do on Saturday?*

Notice the question words (WHAT, WHERE, WHEN, HOW) with GOING TO:

| | Are you going to study on Saturday? | No, I'm not. |

WHAT   are you going to do on Saturday?

Are you going to go to the movies?   No, I'm not.

WHERE   are you going to go?

Are you going to buy the tickets today?   No, I'm not.

WHEN   are you going to buy the tickets?

Are you going to travel by bus?   No, I'm not.

HOW   are you going to travel?

Use the appropriate question word at the beginning of a question.

1 Construct mini-dialogues using the words in italics and the pictures as cues.

Is he going to study *geography*?
No, he's not.
What is he going to study?
Mathematics.

Are they going to send the hat *tomorrow*?
No, they're not.
When are they going to send it?
Tuesday.

Are you going to *read*?
No, I'm not.
What are you going to do?
Ski.

Are we going to see *the museum*?

_____ .

_____ ?

_____ .

Are you going to read *the letter*?

_____ .

_____ ?

_____ .

Is she going to be *at the picnic*?

_____ .

_____ ?

_____ .

Is the program going to start *at two o'clock*?

_____ .

_____ ?

_____ .

Is he going to go *by car*?

_____ .

_____ ?

_____ .

Are they going to eat *at the restaurant*?

_____ .

_____ ?

_____ .

2 Answer the questions according to the pictures. Bill and Janet are going to go to the city.

a.

b.

c.

d.

e.

f.

g.

a.　**Where are Bill and Janet going to shop?**
→ **They're going to shop on King Street.**

b.　**When are they going to go?**
→ **They're going to go on Tuesday.**

c.　How are they going to go?

d.　What is Bill going to buy?

e.　What is Janet going to buy?

f.　When are they going to eat lunch?

g.　When are they going to go home?

83

3 Answer the questions according to the picture.

Who is going to teach Victor and Philip?
→ Vincent is going to teach them.

What is he going to teach them?

When is he going to teach them, at night or after school?

What are they going to play?

Where are they going to play, in the park or at school?

Who is going to play with them?

Subject questions with GOING TO: *Who is going to play?*

Notice the use of WHO and WHAT as subjects:

WHO | is | going to buy tickets?
I | am going to buy tickets.

WHO | is | going to play?
They | are going to play.

WHAT | is | going to help him?
This book | is going to help him.

Use WHO for persons and WHAT for things. Use the statement pattern for subject questions. Remember that BE is always singular in subject questions:

They are going to leave now.

Who IS going to leave now?

Change to subject questions with *who* or *what*, using the cues.

Paul **is going to write a letter. / the notes?**
→ **Who is going to write the notes?**

The news **is going to make us happy. / sad?**
→ **What is going to make us sad?**

My father is going to give us the pictures. / the record?

John is going to wash the car. / the dishes?

He is going to play. / study?

The hat is going to be black. / white?

The net is going to be five dollars. / ten dollars?

We are going to play volleyball. / football?

John is going to teach us the game. / the song?

86

General questions with HAPPEN: *What happened at the party?*

Use WHAT plus the verb HAPPEN to ask general questions. You are asking for complete information: *What happens at Christmas? What happened last night?*

What is happening?

a. Ann

b. Henry and Joe

c. Jack

d. Linda

e. The boys

f. He

g. Alice

h. Gilles

a.   Ann is playing basketball.

b. _____ .

c. _____ .

d. _____ .

e. _____ .

f. _____ .

g. _____ .

h. _____ .

1 Nathan and Keith

N.: What are you going to do
this afternoon?

K.: I'm going to play basketball at the gym.

N.: Aren't you going to be at Bill's house at 4:30?

K.: Yes, but I'm going to be late. First I'm going to
take my sister to her piano lesson. Then I'm
going to Bill's house.

2 Joan and Wanda

J.: What happened yesterday?

W.: My friend and I went to the
new shopping center.

J.: Did you like it?

W.: Oh, yes. It's beautiful and it has many stores.

J.: What did you do there?

W.: We shopped for winter clothes. I bought a coat,
and my friend bought two dresses.

3 Read the story and prepare a dialogue between Diane and Christine.

Many things happened in school yesterday. The history teacher gave us a quiz in Canadian history. It was very difficult. After the quiz the teacher showed us a film on Old Montreal. In the afternoon the English teacher read a short story by Edgar Allan Poe. It was very interesting.

Diane: What happened in school yesterday?

Christine: The history teacher...

Continue the dialogue.

READ

Christmas is next month. The radio stations are going to play Christmas music. The stores are going to be very busy. Some people are already doing their Christmas shopping.

Many families have Christmas trees in their homes. We are going to buy our tree a few days before Christmas.

First, we make or buy presents. I'm going to buy a pen for my brother. He is always writing letters. For my little sister I'm going to make a toy. All of us are going to buy our mother a bracelet. That is going to be her Christmas present.

On Christmas Eve we are going to put up the tree in the living room and then decorate it. We use small electric lights and other decorations. Then we put the presents under the tree. We don't open them until Christmas morning.

Answer the questions.

1. When is Christmas?

2. What are the radio stations going to play?

3. What are people going to do?

4. How are the stores going to be?

5. What do many families have in their homes at Christmas?

6. What is the writer going to buy for his brother?

7. What is the writer going to make for his sister?

8. What are they going to do on Christmas Eve?

9. What happens Christmas morning?

THINK

What are they going to do for Christmas?

PRONOUNCE

Contrast [t] and [θ].

tree [t]	three [θ]
	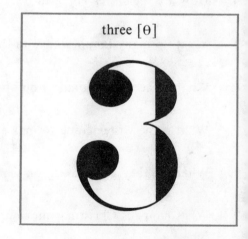

92

tennis	sister	Kenneth	birthday
tell	hospital	think	Kathleen
Toronto	want	month	teeth
ticket	last	thanks	thirsty
tree	wet	thirteen	Thursday

Ted, did you sell your ticket for the game?
Yes. Edith gave me three dollars for it.

Was Kenneth sick last month?
Yes. He was in the hospital for thirteen days.

We ate spaghetti and pizza at the restaurant. After the pizza I was thirsty.
I ordered a soda.

UNIT 6

CONVERSATION

Identifying a person.

Vincent:

Charles, look at the people on the steps.

Is that Nancy with them?

Charles:

Which one?

Vincent:

The tall one.

Charles:

The one with the suitcase?

Vincent:

No. The one with the package.

Charles:

Yes. That's Nancy.

Vincent:

Hello, Nancy! How was your trip?

Nancy:

Fine! We had a very good flight.

ADAPTATION

Construct new sentences like the models using the cues.

people on the steps.

Nancy?

Look at the people on the steps.

Is that Nancy with them?

girls in the house.

_____ .

Paula?

_____ ?

men at the door.

_____ .

Dr. Collins?

_____ ?

teachers in the classroom.

_____ .

Miss Smith?

_____ ?

players in the stadium.

_____ .

John?

_____ ?

suitcase?

package.

Nancy.

Which one? The one with the suitcase?

No. The one with the package.

Yes. That's Nancy.

black dress?

white pants.

Kathleen.

_____ ? _____ ?

_____ . _____ .

_____ . _____ .

short hair.

long hair.

Joe.

_____ ? _____ ?

_____ . _____ .

_____ . _____ .

books?

flowers.

Mrs. Jones.

_____ ? _____ ?

_____ . _____ .

_____ . _____ .

cat? _____ ? _____ ?

dog. _____ . _____ .

Dennis. _____ . _____ .

3

Nancy! trip?

Hello, Nancy! How was your trip?

flight.

Fine! We had a very good flight.

Jim! evening? _____ ! _____ ?

dinner. _____ ! _____ .

Patricia! vacation? _____ ! _____ ?

trip. _____ ! _____ .

Ethel! party? _____ ! _____ ?

time. _____ ! _____ .

Vincent! class? _____ ! _____ ?

teacher. _____ ! _____ .

Prepositional phrases: *He is sitting at the table.*

Notice the meaning of UNDER, OVER, AT, ON, IN and the
position of the prepositional phrases:

A cat is UNDER THE TABLE. It is black.
→ The cat UNDER THE TABLE is black.

A light is OVER THE TABLE. It is electric.
→ The light OVER THE TABLE is electric.

A boy is AT THE TABLE. He is John.
→ The boy AT THE TABLE is John.

Some spaghetti is ON THE TABLE. It is hot.
→ The spaghetti ON THE TABLE is hot.

Some milk is IN THE PITCHER. It is cold.
→ The milk IN THE PITCHER is cold.

The prepositional phrase can occur directly after the verb, or
in combined sentences after the noun it modifies.

1 Combine each pair of sentences into one.

A cat is under the table. The cat is black.
→ **The cat under the table is black.**

Some water is in the pitcher. The water is cold.
→ **The water in the pitcher is cold.**

A suitcase is on the table. The suitcase is mine.

A woman is on the plane. The woman is Mrs. Collins.

A boy is at the door. The boy is my friend.

A net is on the beach. The net is John's.

A man is under the tree. The man is Mr. Coleman.

A girl is at the window. The girl is Helen.

A picture is on the wall. The picture is a photograph.

2 Ask and answer questions about the picture. Use the prepositions *under, over, at, on,* and *in*.

Is the cat under the table or over it?
→ **The cat is under the table.**

Is the pitcher on the table or under it?
→ **The pitcher is on the table.**

_____ ?

_____ .

_____ ?

_____ .

_____ ?

_____ .

99

Prepositional phrases: *The car is in front of the school*.

Notice the use of IN FRONT OF, IN BACK OF, NEAR, FAR FROM, BETWEEN:

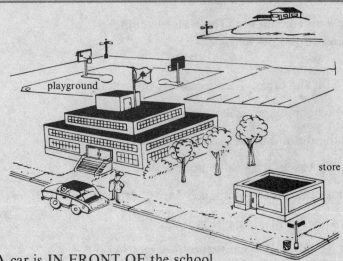

A car is IN FRONT OF the school.
The car is small.
→ The car IN FRONT OF the school is small.

A playground is IN BACK OF the school.
The playground is big.
→ The playground IN BACK OF the school is big.

A store is NEAR the school.
The store is new.
→ The store NEAR the school is new.

A house is FAR FROM the school.
The house is my house.
→ The house FAR FROM the school is my house.

Some trees are BETWEEN the store and the school.
The trees are tall.
→ The trees BETWEEN the store and the school are tall.

1 Ask and answer questions about the picture.

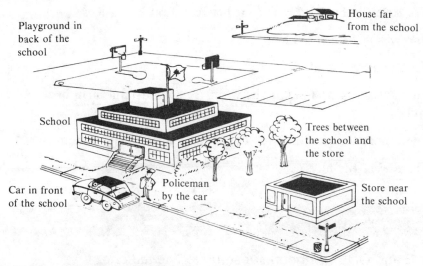

Playground in back of the school

House far from the school

School

Trees between the school and the store

Car in front of the school

Policeman by the car

Store near the school

Where is the car, in front of the school or in back of it?
→ **The car is in front of the school.**

Where is the house, near the school or far from it?
→ **The house is far from the school.**

2 Answer the questions individually according to the picture.

SCHOOL CAFETERIA

Rose

Helen

Frank

Paul

John

What was John doing, standing in line or walking?
→ **He was standing in line.**

Where was he standing, in back of Paul or in front of him?
→ He was standing in back of Paul.

Where was Rose waiting, in back of Helen or in front of her?

Was Helen in back of Frank, or between Frank and Rose?

Who was in front of John?

Was John by the table?

Where was Frank standing, between Helen and Paul or in back of Paul?

Where were the girls, in back of the boys or in front of them?

Where were the boys?

STUDY 3

ONE and ONES as noun substitutes: *The tall one.*

Notice the use of ONE and ONES:

John has two books, a red *book* and a green *book*.
→ John has two books, a red ONE and a green ONE.

I see two boys, a tall *boy* and a short *boy*.
→ I see two boys, a tall ONE and a short ONE.

I saw three boys, a tall *boy*, a *boy* with red hair, and a *boy* with a hat.
→ I saw three boys; a tall ONE, ONE with red hair, and ONE with a hat.

I knew all the boys, the *boys* in school and the *boys* near my house.
→ I knew all the boys, the ONES in school and the ONES near my house.

Use ONE and ONES in place of a noun to avoid repetition.

Answer the questions according to the pictures. Use *one* or *ones*.
Violet and Margaret are going to Mary's party. They are talking about it.

a.

b.

c.

d.

e.

f.

a. **Are you going to wear the black coat or the white coat?**
→ **I'm going to wear the black one.**

b. Are you going to wear the black shoes or the white shoes?

c. Are you going to buy the short dress or the long dress?

d. Are you going to go with the tall boy or the short boy?

e. Is he going to wear a new coat or an old coat?

f. Are you going to give Mary red roses or white roses?

WHICH in questions: *Which one is John?*

Notice the use of WHICH in the questions:

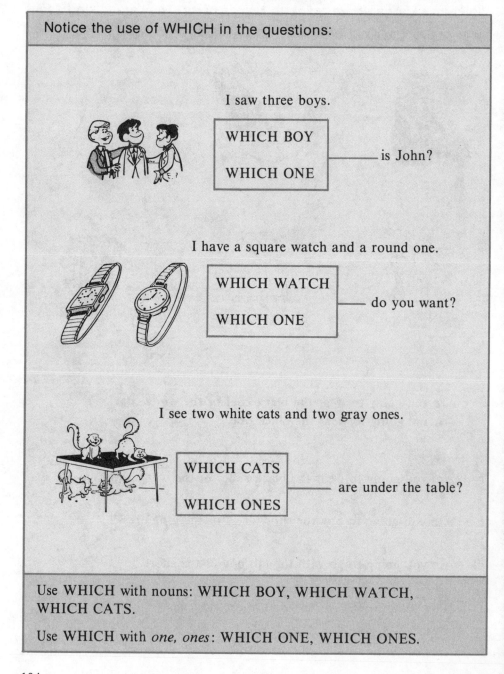

I saw three boys.

| WHICH BOY |
| WHICH ONE | is John?

I have a square watch and a round one.

| WHICH WATCH |
| WHICH ONE | do you want?

I see two white cats and two gray ones.

| WHICH CATS |
| WHICH ONES | are under the table?

Use WHICH with nouns: WHICH BOY, WHICH WATCH, WHICH CATS.

Use WHICH with *one, ones*: WHICH ONE, WHICH ONES.

Construct mini-dialogues using the cues.

I made two pies. Bill ate one of them.

                        Which one did he eat?

small.

                        The small one.

Helen sang three songs. We liked two of them.

                        Which ones did you like?

French.

                        The French ones.

Fred saw three watches. He bought one of them.

                        _____ ?

square.

                        _____ .

He saw two girls. He remembered one of them.

                        _____ ?

tall.

                        _____ .

I saw four boys near the school.
One was John.

_____ ?

short.

_____ .

We had two things to do. We
did only one. we d

_____ ?

important.

_____ .

They saw two taxis. They took
one of them.

_____ ?

yellow.

_____ .

Jane saw many hats. She
bought three of them.

_____ ?

white.

_____ .

He wrote three letters. I read
two of them.

_____ ?

long.

_____ .

106

They watched two programs.
She watched only one. _____ ?

interesting. _____ .

1 Kenneth, Linda and Ethel

L.: Kenneth, look at those girls near the car.
     Is that Ethel with them?

K.: Which one?

L.: The one with the glasses.

K.: Yes. That's Ethel.

L.: Hello, Ethel!

E.: Hello, Linda! Hello, Kenneth,

2 Peter and John

P.: Where's Bill?

J.: He's in line. Do you see him?

P.: Is he the one with the black pants?

J.: No. 'He's the one with the brown shirt.

P.: Oh, I see him. He's standing between Alfred and Nancy.

READ

Bill and Kenneth visit Mr. Collins every Sunday. Mr. Collins lives in a small house far from the city. His house is near a lake. In the afternoon they go fishing. In back of the lake is a forest. It is fall now and the leaves are yellow, red and brown. Bill likes the yellow ones, and Kenneth likes the red ones.

Last Sunday the two boys visited Mr. Collins. At five o'clock Bill, Kenneth and Mr. Collins returned to the house. They had fish for dinner that night. After dinner they sat in front of the fireplace and told jokes. At nine o'clock Kenneth and Bill went home by train.

Answer the questions.

1. When do Bill and Kenneth visit Mr. Collins?

2. Where does Mr. Collins live?

3. Is his house far from a lake?

4. What is in back of the lake?

5. What happens in the fall?

6. Which leaves does Bill like?

7. Which ones does Kenneth like?

8. What did they do after dinner last Sunday?

9. What happened at nine o'clock?

10. How did they go home?

Where is the...?

Tell where each thing is in relation to the other things in the picture. (e.g. The horse is *behind* the house. The bus is *far from* the city.)

Contrast [ð] and [θ].

either [ð]	ether [θ]
	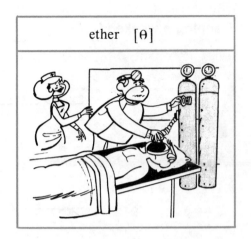

this	father	Smith	Elizabeth
brother	they	Ethel	Catherine
that	mother	theater	think
those	the	tooth	mouth

How many teeth does the baby have?
My brother Kenneth has only three.
When is his birthday?
Next month.

Where is the St. Catherine Theater?
It's at Thirteen-thirty Smith Street.
Isn't this Thirteen-thirty Smith Street?
No, it isn't. This is Elizabeth Street.

UNIT 7

CONVERSATION

Planning a weekend.

Diane:

Allen, what do you like to do on weekends?

Allen:

I like to go out, but sometimes I have to work.

Diane:

Where do you like to go?

Allen:

To the movies.

Diane:

We're going to Mount Orford next weekend.

Do you want to come?

Allen:

No, thank you. I have to help my father.

Construct new sentences like the models using the cues.

1

Allen, on weekends?

Allen, what do you like to do on weekends?

go out, work.

I like to go out, but sometimes I have to work.

Bill, on Saturday?

_____ ?

play soccer, study.

_____ .

Linda, at night?

_____ ?

play the piano, write letters.

_____ .

Helen, in the evening?

_____ ?

go to the movies, stay home.

_____ .

Steven, in the afternoon?

_____ ?

play ping-pong, wash the car.

_____ .

2

Mount Orford, weekend.

We're going to Mount Orford next weekend.

you?

Do you want to come?

Winnipeg, year.

_____ .

they?

_____ ?

game, week.

_____ .

he?

_____ ?

movies, Thursday.

_____ .

she?

_____ ?

circus, Friday.

_____ .

you?

_____ ?

3

stay home.

I'm going to stay home.

help my father.

I have to help my father.

be at school.

_____ .

practice soccer.

_____ .

stay at the office.

_____ .

work tonight.

_____ .

114

drive to the airport.   _____ .

meet a friend.   _____ .

stay at the library.   _____ .

study biology.   _____ .

STUDY 1

Verb combinations with VERB + TO + VERB: *I like to go out*.

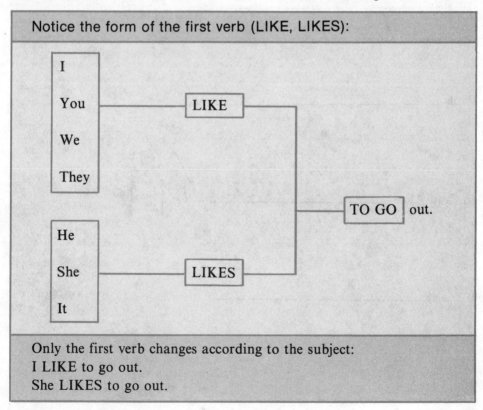

Notice the form of the first verb (LIKE, LIKES):

I
You
We
They
LIKE

He
She
It
LIKES

TO GO out.

Only the first verb changes according to the subject:
I LIKE to go out.
She LIKES to go out.

What do these people like to do?

They like to sing.

John _____ .

His sister _____ .

Paul _____ .

Joe and Alice _____ .

I _____ .

They _____ .

116

He _____ .

We _____ .

Sentences with VERB + TO + VERB: *Where do you like to go? Do you want to come?*

Compare the sentences with simple verbs and the sentences with VERB + TO + VERB:

Do you | have to work | this evening? | Yes, I do.
Do you | have | a new car? | No, I don't.

What does he | want to do? | He | wants to see | Peter.
What does he | want? | He | wants | a new bicycle.

Where do you | want to go | on Sunday?
Where do you | eat |

Does Karen | want to buy | a new bicycle?
Does Karen | want |

Doesn't she | like to see | movies?
Doesn't she | like |

The construction VERB + TO + VERB follows the same rules as for simple verbs.

117

1 Change to yes/no questions with *do* or *does*. Use the pictures as cues.

He doesn't like to play the piano.
→ Does he like to play the guitar?

She doesn't want to go to the beach.
→ Does she want to go to the city?

I don't want to study geography.

They don't have to play soccer.

Jane doesn't want to stay in Montreal.

Bill doesn't like to read newspapers.

I don't have to dance tomorrow.

John doesn't want to go alone.

Linda

2 The two women are jogging and talking. Complete the dialogue using short answers.

Do you get up at 7 every morning?

Yes, I do.

Does Paul have to get up early too?

No, he doesn't.

Do you have to go shopping every day?

X

Do your children like to eat breakfast early?

Did you and Paul go to the concert last night?

Do you like to jog?

X

119

3 Construct mini-dialogues using the pictures as cues.

Do you want to play *tennis*?
No, I don't.
What do you want to play?
I want to play baseball.

John

Did *they* **have to work hard?**
No, they didn't.
Who had to work hard?
John had to work hard.

Does Philip like to read *astronomy*?
No, he doesn't.
What does he like to read?
He likes to read history.

Do you want to watch *the movie*?

_____ .

_____ ?

_____ .

Did *Joan* have to wash the dishes?

_____ .

_____ ?

Michael

_____ .

Did your parents want to go *to Europe*?

_____ .

_____ ?

_____ .

Do Frank and Henry like to study *in the afternoon*?

_____ .

_____ ?

_____ .

Does *Mrs. Newton* plan to live in Alberta?

_____ .

_____ ?

Mrs. Smith

_____ .

Did you want to go *to the store*?

_____ .

_____ ?

_____ .

USED TO: *Where did they use to go? They used to go to the park.*

Notice the forms USED TO and USE TO:

What DID John USE TO do?
→ He USED TO go to the movies.

DID he USE TO go often?
→ Yes, he DID. (No, he DIDN'T.)

Who DID he USE TO go with? DID he USE TO go alone?
→ No. He DIDN'T USE TO go alone. He USED TO go with me.

USED TO indicates habitual activity in the past. Use the simple form (USE) with DID in questions and negatives.

1 Change to statements in the past with *used to*. Use the pictures as cues.

I play tennis.
→ **I used to play hockey.**

They go to the theater.
→ **They used to go to the movies.**

My parents travel in the winter.

Daniel

She likes Paul.

England

He lives in France.

123

We ski in the Laurentians.

My sister is a doctor.

I get up at 7.

They take the train to work.

2 Change to yes/no questions using the given cue.

Margaret used to practice the piano. / guitar?
→ **Did she use to practice the guitar?**

John used to play basketball. / baseball?
→ **Did he use to play baseball?**

My brother used to watch television. / the news?

Helen used to get up early. / at seven?

My sister used to walk to school. / the game?

Steven and Rose used to go to the movies. / the theater?

Frank used to play the guitar. / piano?

We used to memorize dialogues. / poems?

My parents used to travel in the summer. / July?

3 Ask the correct information question and give the answer. Use the pictures as cues.

What did Mary use to like?

Mary used to like television.

Who used to work hard?

Jane   Paul

Jane and Paul used to work hard.

_____ ?   used to like the nurse.

_____ ?   John used to sleep late

_____ ?   They used to visit their friends

_____ ?   Bill used to play

126

_____ ?   Bob   David   used to tell jokes.

_____ ?   Mr. Johnson used to work

SPEAK

1 Dale and Anthony

D.: What did you do yesterday afternoon?

A.: I worked. I had to help my father at the store.

D.: Do you like to help your father?

A.: Yes, I do. I like to play football with him, too. He used to be a famous football player.

127

2 Alexander, Claudia, and Violet

A.: Good morning. What do you have to do today?

C.: We have to work at the library. We're trying to make some money.

A.: How do you want to use it?

V.: I want to go to the United States, and Claudia wants to buy a new tennis racket.

READ

Daniel is giving a talk in English class.

Let's discuss sports. First I want to talk about volleyball. North Americans play volleyball with a big ball and a high net. In this game the six players on one team try to hit the ball over the net. The other team has to hit it back.

We play basketball with a big ball and two baskets. The five players on each team try to throw the ball in their basket. Many men, women and children like to watch basketball games.

In hockey the six players on each team hit a puck with their sticks. They try to shoot it into a net and get goals. The goalie of the other team has to stop the puck.

I like to participate in all sports.

Answer the questions:

1.   What is Daniel doing in class?

2.   What does he want to talk about first?

3.   What do the players try to do in volleyball? In basketball?

4.   What do many men, women and children like to do?

5.   What do hockey players do with their sticks?

6.   What do they try to get?

7. What does the goalie have to do?

8. What does Daniel like to do?

9. Do you like to participate in sports? Which ones?

THINK

What do they like to do?

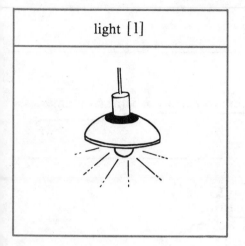

light [1]

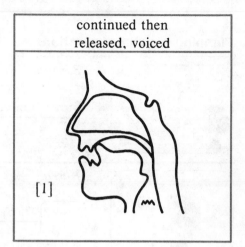

continued then
released, voiced

[1]

like	Philip	well	people
class	college	cold	bottle
please	telephone	lettuce	Daniel
blue	usually	motel	animal
English	hello	mail	always

What's in the bottle on the table?

Milk.

Are we going to eat lunch now?

No. We have to wait for Sally.

She's always late.

We looked at the animals in the zoo. Philip liked the lions. They have long tails. Donald loved the elephants. We saw a little one. It was a baby elephant.

UNIT 8

Planning a summer vacation.

Barbara:

Karen, I'm going to go to Gaspé next summer.

Karen:

Wow! That's terrific!

Barbara:

How many suitcases do I have to take?

Karen:

Take two — a big one and a small one.

Barbara:

How much money do I need?

Karen:

A lot. About five hundred dollars.

132

Barbara:

Are there many interesting places to visit?

Karen:

Yes, there are. There are beautiful mountains and famous beaches.

ADAPTATION

Construct new sentences like the models using the cues.

| 1 |

| --- |

Gaspé, summer.　　　　**I'm going to go to Gaspé next summer.**

terrific!　　　　**That's terrific!**

Ottawa, week.　　　　_____ .

nice!　　　　_____ !

the museum, Sunday.　　　　_____ .

interesting!　　　　_____ !

the beach, weekend.　　　　_____ .

fun!　　　　_____ !

the theater, Friday.   ———————————————— .

expensive!   ———————————————— !

2

suitcases, take?   **How many suitcases do I have to take?**

big, small.   **Take two — a big one and a small one.**

songs, sing?   ———————————————— ?

funny, sad.   ———————————————— .

dialogues, memorize?   ———————————————— ?

easy, difficult.   ———————————————— .

letters, write?   ———————————————— ?

long, short.   ———————————————— .

shirts, buy?   ———————————————— ?

blue, white.   ———————————————— .

3

money?   **How much money do I need?**
five hundred dollars.   **A lot. About five hundred dollars.**

sugar?   ———————————————— ?

ten kilos.   ———————— . ————————

134

milk?

twelve litres.

_____ ?

_____ . _____ .

time?

forty hours.

_____ ?

_____ . _____ .

paper?

two thousand sheets.

_____ ?

_____ . _____ .

4

interesting?

Are there many interesting places to visit?

mountains, beaches.

Yes, there are. There are mountains and beaches.

beautiful?

_____ ?

monuments, palaces.

_____ . _____ .

important?

_____ ?

museums, national parks.

_____ . _____ .

famous?

_____ ?

churches, universities.

_____ . _____ .

HOW MANY and HOW MUCH with count nouns and mass nouns: *How many suitcases do I have to take? How much money do I need?*

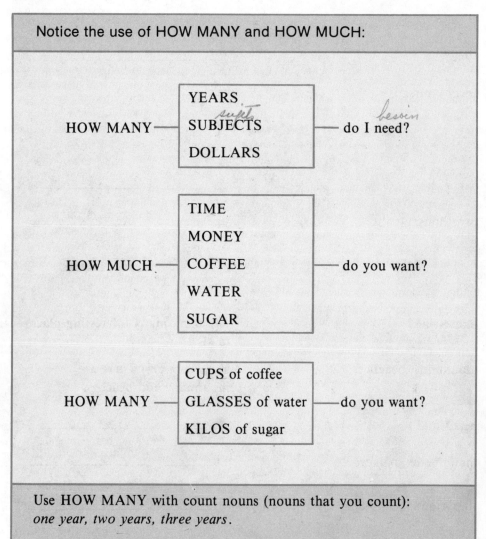

Notice the use of HOW MANY and HOW MUCH:

HOW MANY — YEARS / SUBJECTS / DOLLARS — do I need?

HOW MUCH — TIME / MONEY / COFFEE / WATER / SUGAR — do you want?

HOW MANY — CUPS of coffee / GLASSES of water / KILOS of sugar — do you want?

Use HOW MANY with count nouns (nouns that you count): *one year, two years, three years*.

Use HOW MUCH with mass nouns (nouns that you cannot count): *time, coffee, water*.

Mass nouns are countable in units: *a cup of coffee, two glasses of water, three kilos of sugar*.

1 Ask and answer questions using the cues. Change count nouns to the plural.

money   How much money do you want?
a lot   I want a lot of money.

paper   How much paper do you want?
a lot   I want a lot of paper.

dollar   How many dollars do you want?
ten   I want ten dollars.

eraser ————————————— ?
six   —————————————— .

book —————————————— ?
twenty ————————————— .

water —————————————— ?
a lot —————————————— .

sugar —————————————— ?
a lot —————————————— .

pen   —————————————— ?
one   —————————————— .

coffee ————————————— ?
a lot —————————————— .

time   —————————————— ?
a lot —————————————— .

2 Ask the questions with *how much* or *how many*.

I need some money.
How much money do you need?
About two thousand dollars.
How many dollars?
About two thousand.

I need some erasers.
How many erasers do you need?
Four or five.
How many erasers?
Four or five.

I want some water.

_____ ?

Two or three glasses.

_____ ?

Two or three.

I need some time.

_____ ?

About four or five years.

_____ ?

About four or five.

I have to study some subjects.

_____ ? ,

Seven subjects.

_____ ?

Seven.

We don't have much time.

_____ ?

A few minutes.

_____ ?

A few.

I play some instruments.

_____ ?

Three instruments.

_____ ?

Three.

The library has many books.

_____ ?

About five thousand books.

_____ ?

About five thousand.

My mother needs some rice.

_____ ?

Two boxes.

_____ ?

Two.

Irregular plurals: *child* → *children*.

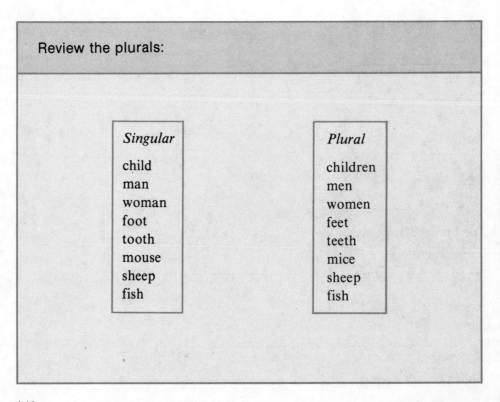

Review the plurals:

Singular	Plural
child	children
man	men
woman	women
foot	feet
tooth	teeth
mouse	mice
sheep	sheep
fish	fish

Complete the mini-dialogues.

She saw a child.
How many children did she see?
One.

I helped two men.
How many men did you help?
Two.

I saw a woman in the store.

_____ did you see _____ ?

_____ .

I found a shark's tooth.

_____ ?

_____ .

They want a fish.

_____ ?

_____ .

Helen had a mouse.

_____ ?

_____ .

He bought three sheep.

_____ ?

_____ .

THERE + BE: *Are there places to visit? There are beaches and mountains.*

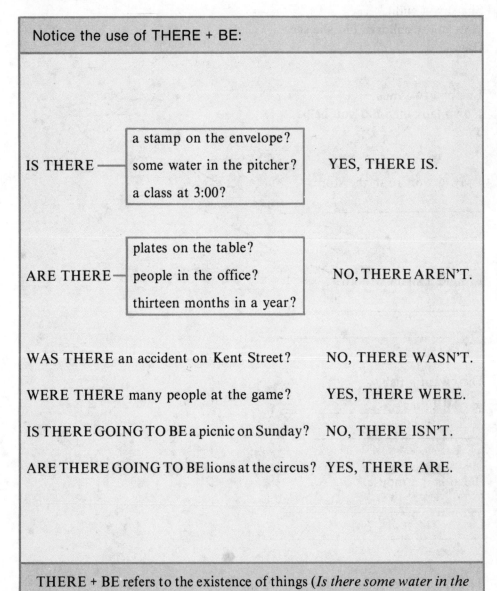

Notice the use of THERE + BE:

IS THERE —— a stamp on the envelope? / some water in the pitcher? / a class at 3:00? YES, THERE IS.

ARE THERE — plates on the table? / people in the office? / thirteen months in a year? NO, THERE AREN'T.

WAS THERE an accident on Kent Street? NO, THERE WASN'T.

WERE THERE many people at the game? YES, THERE WERE.

IS THERE GOING TO BE a picnic on Sunday? NO, THERE ISN'T.

ARE THERE GOING TO BE lions at the circus? YES, THERE ARE.

THERE + BE refers to the existence of things (*Is there some water in the pitcher?*), a true fact (*Are there twelve months in a year?*), or an event that happens (*Was there an accident on Kent Street?*).

Answer the questions according to the picture.

Are there many people in the dining room?
→ No, there aren't.

Are there plates on the table?
→ Yes, there are.

Is there going to be a party tonight?

Is there wine in the glasses?

Are there flowers in the vase?

Are there seven chairs at the table?

Are there going to be six people at the dinner?

Is there going to be music at the party?

1 Margaret and Rachel

M.: Rachel, Frances wants to be a doctor. What do you think?

R.: That's fine. My sister is a doctor, and she likes it very much.

M.: How many years did your sister study?

R.: Six or seven. Seven years, I think. Now she works in the city hospital.

2 Frank and Charles

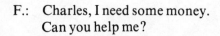

F.: Charles, I need some money. Can you help me?

C.: Yes. How much do you need?

F.: Oh, about fifteen dollars.

C.: What are you going to do with it?

F.: I want to buy a present for my father. Tomorrow is his birthday.

Eleanor's mother is sick. Eleanor is going to buy groceries today. First, she thinks about her grocery list. How much milk does she need? How much bread? How much coffee? How much lettuce? How many tomatoes?

Next, Eleanor makes her list. She is planning to buy two chickens, one head of lettuce and four tomatoes. She's going to need one litre of milk and a loaf of bread too.

Then she thinks about money. How much money does she need? Five dollars? No. She needs about ten dollars. That's a lot, but grocery shopping is expensive.

Answer the questions.

1. What is Eleanor going to do?

2. What does she think about first?

3. How many chickens does she want to buy?

4. How much lettuce does she need?

5. How many litres of milk is she going to need?

6. How much bread does she need?

7. How much money does she need?

Ask and answer questions about the pictures, using *how much* or *how many*. (e.g. *How much money does he need* (*want*)? *He needs* (*wants*) *five dollars*.)

right [r]

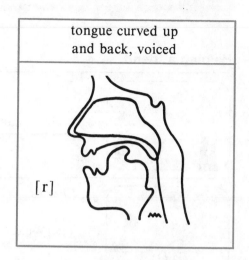

tongue curved up
and back, voiced

[r]

right	library	memorize	sharp
red	Montreal	interesting	store
friend	arrive	bacteria	airport
train	very	during	are
program	story	electric	hour

Henry reads three books a month. He brings home many books from the library. Friday he read about factories in France.

Alfred and Maria went to the Green Tree Restaurant on Front Street. They ate frogs' legs, rice, and French bread. They drank tea. Then they had ice cream.

Margaret and Catherine took a trip to Vancouver in the spring. They traveled by train. They rode for fourteen hours. Margaret brought a diary. She wrote in it every day.

UNIT 9

Helping a friend.

Henry:

Charles, can you help me for a minute?

Charles:

Yes. What can I do?

Henry:

I'm wrapping a gift, and I can't tie it.

Charles:

You need more ribbon. Shall I look for some?

Henry:

Yes, please. And will you bring the scissors too?

Charles:

All right. I'll try to find them.

Henry:

Look in my desk. They might be there.

ADAPTATION

Construct new sentences like the models using the cues.

help me for a minute?
do?

Can you help me for a minute?
Yes. What can I do?

sing for me?

_____ ?

sing?

_____ . _____ ?

read to me?

_____ ?

read?

_____ . _____ ?

work with me?

_____ ?

do?

_____ . _____ ?

play the piano for me?

_____ ?

play?

_____ . _____ ?

string.
look for?

**You need more string.
Shall I look for some?**

paper.

buy?

_____ .

_____ ?

ink.

get?

_____ .

_____ ?

sugar.

ask for?

_____ .

_____ ?

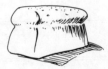

bread.

make?

_____ .

_____ ?

150

3

the scissors?
find.

Will you bring the scissors too?
All right. I'll try to find them.

the knife?

get.

_____ ?

____ . ____ .

the address?

copy.

_____ ?

____ . ____ .

the records?

find.

_____ ?

____ . ____ .

4

desk. They.

Look in my desk. They might
be there.

pocket. It.

____ . ____ .

apartment. She.

____ . ____ .

suitcase. It.

____ . ____ .

office. He.

____ . ____ .

151

The modal auxiliary CAN: *Can you help me?*

Notice the position of CAN:

| I You We They ·He She It | CAN CANNOT/CAN'T | push the car. |

CAN is placed between the subject and the verb. It does not change according to the subject. The negative of CAN is CANNOT or CAN'T.

Notice the meaning of CAN:

Can you lift the rock?

Yes, I can.

Can I eat?

No, you can't.

CAN means ability (*Can you lift the rock? Yes, I can.*) or permission (*Can I eat? No, you can't.*).

1 Respond to each statement using the cue in a negative
sentence.

John can play basketball well. / soccer.
→ **Yes, but he can't play soccer well.**

Edith can recite the alphabet easily. / story.
→ **Yes, but she can't recite the story easily.**

We can watch television tonight. / the game.

I can go home this weekend. / to Montreal.

The doctor can go to the hospital tonight. / to the theater.

She can visit her friend tomorrow. / cousin.

Alexander can play the piano. / violin.

The students can remember the lesson. / dialogue.

2 Construct mini-dialogues using the word and picture cues.

John can play basketball. / tennis?
Can he play tennis?
Yes, he can.

Martha can buy a new coat. / dress?
Can she buy a new dress?
No, she can't.

Paul can sing well. / dance well?

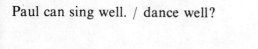

_____ ?

_____ .

Victor can play volleyball. / baseball?

_____ ?

_____ .

Ann can change ten dollars. / twenty dollars?

_____ ?

_____ .

Charles can ride a bicycle. / motorcycle?

_____ ?

_____ .

Michael can skate well. / ski well?

_____ ?

_____ .

Jean can learn to play the guitar. / piano?

_____ ?

_____ .

Victor can go by train. / plane?

_____ ?

_____ .

154

Answer according to the picture.

Bill's friends are having a talent show. What can they do?

Can Philip sing or dance?
→ He can sing.

Can John be the acrobat or the clown?

Can Susan make the dresses or sell the tickets?

Can Elizabeth recite a poem or announce the program?

Can Robert close the curtain or help Susan with the tickets?

Can James play the violin or the drums?

The modal auxiliaries WILL, MIGHT, MUST: *Will we leave at 7?*

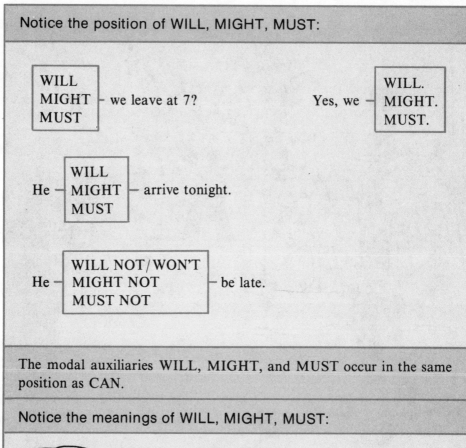

Notice the position of WILL, MIGHT, MUST:

| WILL MIGHT MUST | – we leave at 7? |

Yes, we – WILL. MIGHT. MUST.

He – | WILL MIGHT MUST | – arrive tonight.

He – | WILL NOT/WON'T MIGHT NOT MUST NOT | – be late.

The modal auxiliaries WILL, MIGHT, and MUST occur in the same position as CAN.

Notice the meanings of WILL, MIGHT, MUST:

It will rain tomorrow.

It might bite.

You must stay in bed.

WILL refers to the future; MIGHT to a possibility; MUST to an obligation.

1 Change to negative statements using the cues.

My father will go to Windsor tomorrow. / Toronto.
→ **He will not go to Toronto.**

Philip might see the parade. / circus.
→ **He might not see the circus.**

We must study. / go to the movies.

You will like his house. / her apartment.

Jane can write English. / Italian.

They might buy a house. / car.

My parents must stay home. / go out.

My sister will go to the movies alone. / with Peter.

2 Change to yes/no questions using the cues. Then answer according to the pictures.

You can watch TV in the bedroom. / living room?
Can I watch TV in the living room?
Yes, you can.

My father will buy a new radio. / TV?
Will he buy a new TV?
No, he won't.

157

I might go to Quebec. / Montreal?
Might you go to Montreal?
Yes, I might.

Mary must clean the garage. / kitchen?

_____ ?

_____ .

I can go to the store now. / at 5 o'clock?

_____ ?

_____ .

She might go to the circus on Sunday. / movies?

_____ ?

_____ .

He will memorize the dialogue. / song?

_____ ?

_____ .

Frank must study at the library. / home?

_____ ?

_____ .

3 Complete the mini-dialogues using *can, will, might, must*.

A.: **We might go to Ontario this summer.**
B.: **<u>Will</u> you visit Ottawa?**

A.: You must do your homework before 7:30.
B.: _____ I go out after?

A.: Will you take a vacation this summer?
B.: Yes. I _____ go to the Maritimes.

A.: I might go to Russia next year.
B.: You _____ need a lot of money.
A.: I know. I have to work hard and I _____ save money.

A.: It might snow tonight.
B.: Terrific! Then we _____ go skiing.
A.: But first we _____ find transportation.

A.: Can you come to the concert with us?
B.: I _____ have a test tomorrow and I _____ study.

The modal auxiliary SHALL: *Shall I look for some ribbon?*

Notice the meaning and use of SHALL:

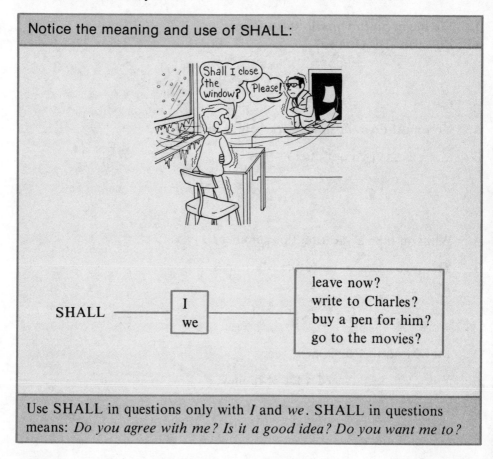

| SHALL | I we | leave now?
write to Charles?
buy a pen for him?
go to the movies? |

Use SHALL in questions only with *I* and *we*. SHALL in questions means: *Do you agree with me? Is it a good idea? Do you want me to?*

PRACTICE

Change the statements to questions using *shall* and *too*.

John will leave now. / I?
→ **Shall I leave now too?**

They will write a letter to Charles. / we?
→ **Shall we write a letter to Charles?**

He will call Henry tonight. / I?

They will go tomorrow. / we?

Peter will sing a song. / I?

Alice and Ann will memorize the poem. / we?

Eve will visit Ann next week. / I?

David will introduce her. / I?

They will eat with John. / we?

SPEAK

1 Helen and Martha

H.: Martha, will you tell me about your family?

M.: Sure. I have a large family: my parents and five brothers and sisters.

H.: Can you tell me something about your parents?

M.: Yes, I can. My mother is a housewife. My father is a mailman. You'll meet them Friday night.

F.: Richard, can you play hockey this afternoon?

R.: No, I can't. I have to stay home.
I must clean my room.

F.: Can't you clean it tomorrow? I'll help you.

R.: No. My cousin is coming tomorrow morning.
He'll be here a week.

F.: Can he play hockey?

R.: Yes, he can.

F.: Good! Will you introduce us?

R.: Of course!

READ

Games can be fun, but they can be difficult too. Scrabble is my favorite game, but it is not an easy one. Charles, Caroline, and I are going to play Scrabble tonight. Caroline cannot play, but I will teach her. Do you know the rules? I will explain them.

Each player must take seven letters. Your letters may be A, S, T, E, B, C, and L. You can spell *table* with these letters. You can also spell *sat, cat, late,* and *bat*. But you must be careful. There are points for each letter in a word.

For example, A = 1, S = 1, T = 1, E = 1, B = 3, C = 3, and L = 1. So the number of points can change from word to word. *Table* will give you seven points, but *sat* will give you only three points, and *cat* will give you five points. Use *table*. You will earn more points and you might win the game. There is one important rule of the game — you cannot use names of people, countries, or cities.

At the end of the game the players must add their points. You might have one hundred forty points. That is a good score. But I might have one hundred sixty points, and Charles might have one hundred seventy. Charles wins.

Shall we play?

Answer the questions.

1. Can games be fun and difficult?

2. How many people are going to play Scrabble tonight?

3. How many letters must each player take?

4. What words can you spell with A, S, T, E, B, C, and L?

5. How many points will *table* give you?

6. How many points will *sat* give you?

7. Can you use the name of a country?

8. What must the players do at the end of the game?

9. Can you play Scrabble?

Helen, John, and Charles are thinking about their plans for the weekend. Tell us about them. Use WILL, MUST, MIGHT, and CAN.

Contrast [l] and [r] .

light [l]	right [r]
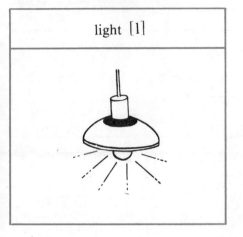	

lake	hello	rice	art
lesson	slowly	bread	dinner
clock	Sally	drink	hour
feel	pencil	Rose	guitar
always	apple	record	translator

Will the children be waiting for me at school?
Yes, they will. Please drive slowly and carefully. Many car accidents happen in the rain.

Shall I call your friends?
Yes, please. They're late for dinner.
I'll call their hotel room. They're probably there.

UNIT 10

CONVERSATION

Planning for a friend's visit.

Carl:

When will your friend arrive?

Virginia:

In fifteen minutes.

Carl:

What shall I call her, Rosemary or Rose?

Virginia:

Rose is fine.

Carl:

Where can we take her?

Virginia:

We can take her to the zoo.

Or she might like to see a movie.

Carl:

Why can't we go to the zoo *and* to a movie?

Virginia:

Because there won't be enough time.

She has to leave Sunday night.

ADAPTATION

Construct new sentences like the models using the cues.

your friend?   **When will your friend arrive?**
In 15 minutes.   **In 15 minutes.**

the train?   _____ ?

At 10:15.   _____ .

your parents?   _____ ?

Next week.   _____ .

his brothers?   _____ ?

Tonight.   _____ .

the package?   _____ ?

Next month.   _____ .

167

call her, Rosemary, Rose?

What shall I call her, Rosemary or Rose?

Rose.

Rose is fine.

give you, coffee, tea?

_____ ?

Tea.

_____ .

buy him, a record, a book?

_____ ?

a book.

_____ .

3

her?

Where can we take her?

zoo. see a movie.

We can take her to the zoo. Or she might like to see a movie.

him?

_____ ?

circus. go to the game.

_____ . _____ .

them?

_____ ?

beach. stay home.

_____ . _____ .

her?

_____ ?

play. watch TV.

_____ . _____ .

168

Paul? _____ ?

movies. listen to music. _____ . _____ .

4

the zoo, a movie?   **Why can't we go to the zoo _and_ to a movie?**

She, Sunday night.   **Because there won't be enough time. She has to leave Sunday night.**

Moncton, Saint John? _____ ?

He, next Tuesday. _____ . _____ .

the beach, the show? _____ ?

They, tonight. _____ . _____ .

the party, the movies? _____ ?

We, at midnight. _____ . _____ .

the dinner, the game? _____ ?

You, early. _____ . _____ .

169

Information questions with modal auxiliaries: *When will your friend arrive?*

Notice the choice and order of the words:

WHAT   SHALL we buy?

SHALL we buy a record?

WHO   CAN you see?

CAN you see the president?

WHERE   MIGHT it be?

MIGHT it be on the desk?

WHEN   MUST he write the test?

MUST he write the test next week?

HOW   WILL they come?

WILL they come by car?

Use the appropriate question word (WHAT, WHO, WHERE, WHEN, HOW) plus the yes/no question form.

1 Provide the correct information question.

Can we go *to Bill's house*? **No.**
→ **Where can we go?**

Shall we go *after work*? **No.**
→ **When shall we go?**

Will we *listen to some records*? **No.**
→ **What will we do?**

Must they *go to the hospital*? No.

Might Richard and Susan be there *early*? No.

Does John want to take *his sister*? No.

Shall I make *some cookies*? No.

Will Helen and I go *by car*? No.

Does she want to go *by bus*? No.

2 Answer the questions according to the pictures.

When can Mary go, Monday or Tuesday?
→ **She can go Tuesday.**

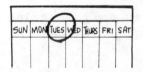

**Where are you going to go, to Nova Scotia or
to New Brunswick?**
→ **I'm going to go to Nova Scotia.**

NOVA SCOTIA

171

What did you do yesterday, study or watch television?
→ **I studied.**

Where is the doctor, at his office or at the hospital?

How do you like your coffee, with milk or with cream?

What must I study, history or mathematics?

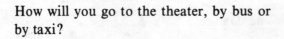

When will you take a vacation, in June or in December?

How will you go to the theater, by bus or by taxi?

Where do you want to study Japanese, here or in Japan?

When must you eat dinner, now or at seven o'clock?

What will you see, a good movie or a game?

STUDY 2

Information questions about the subject: *Who is coming*?

Notice the use of WHO and WHAT as subjects:

WHO   must study?
—
JOHN must study.

WHO   can translate this letter?
—
I   can translate this letter.

WHAT   might happen?
—
An accident might happen.

WHAT will be on TV tonight?
—
The game will be on TV tonight.

WHO and WHAT are the subjects of these questions. They are in the same position as the subjects of the statements.

Provide the correct subject information question with *who* or *what*

What can be fun?　　*Football games* **can be fun.**

_____ ? *John and Bill* will play in today's game.

_____ ? *The game* will begin at two o'clock.

_____ ? *David Martin* can't play hockey today.

_____ ? *Robert* might watch the game on TV.

_____ ? *Susan* must go to the stadium early.

_____ ? *The ticket window* will be open after nine o'clock.

Questions with WHY and answers with BECAUSE: *Why can't we go to the zoo? Because there won't be enough time.*

Notice the use of WHY and BECAUSE:
We must be there before five. → WHY must we be there before five? → BECAUSE they eat dinner early. We can't buy two records. → WHY can't we buy two records? → BECAUSE I have only five dollars. We won't go to David's house today. → WHY won't we go to David's house today? → BECAUSE we don't have enough time.
Use WHY to ask for a cause or reason. Use BECAUSE to give the cause or reason.

Change to questions and answers with *why* and *because*.

We can get up late tomorrow. Tomorrow is Saturday.
→ **Why can we get up late tomorrow?**
→ **Because tomorrow is Saturday.**

He didn't write to you. He didn't remember your address.
→ **Why didn't he write to me?**
→ **Because he didn't remember your address.**

We don't have to go to school today. It's Sunday.

Henry can't go to the movies today. He has to work.

You will like the food here. It's a good restaurant.

Bill visits the hospital often. He wants to be a doctor.

I practice the guitar every day. I want to play on television.

They must practice hockey today. They will play an important game tomorrow.

You can't play in the street. There are many cars.

John can't come to school. He's sick.

Irregular past in [ow]: *write → wrote*.

Learn or review these irregular past forms. Notice the letter and sound changes:

The past tense of

	is	
WRITE		WROTE.
DRIVE		DROVE.
RIDE		RODE.
SPEAK		SPOKE.
BREAK		BROKE.
TELL		TOLD.
SELL		SOLD.

Pronounce these irregular past forms with [ow].

PRACTICE

Answer the questions according to the picture.

What did you break?
→ I broke a window.

How did you break it?

When did you break it?

Who did you tell, Mr. Martin or Mrs. Martin?

What time did you speak to him (her)?

1 Barbara and Eugene

B.: Eugene, are you going to work at the store all day?

E.: Yes. I'll be there from 8:30 to 4:00.

B.: What will you do tonight?

E.: After dinner I'll go to the movies with Sarah Martin. Can you go with us?

B.: Yes. But I must be home by 11:30.

2 Charles and Frank

C.: Hello, Frank. When shall we go to the museum?

F.: I can't go today, Charles. I rode my bicycle to school yesterday, and it broke.

C.: Can't we go by bus?

F.: Yes. But I don't have fifty cents. You'll have to pay for both of us!

3 Martha and Her Sister

M.: Why can't you go to school today?

S.: Because I'm sick.

M.: Why don't you tell Mother?

S.: Because I told her already.

M.: Why doesn't she call Dr. Coleman?

S.: She did. I'll see him at 9 o'clock tomorrow.

Babysitting is an art. A good babysitter has to be a nurse and a cook, but most of all, he or she must love children.

Why do young people babysit? Because they can earn some money, because they want to help a friend, or simply because they love children.

But babysitting is not easy. There are many responsibilities. Babysitters must always be ready for an emergency. A child might get sick or might have an accident and need to go to the hospital. Babysitters must know what to do. They must call the parents in an emergency.

The babysitter needs to ask the parents some important questions: Where will they be? What is the phone number? Where can the children play? What must they eat for supper? What time must they go to bed?

Children usually test a new babysitter. For example, they might ask for a soda or they might want to eat candy before supper. At bedtime, they might want to watch television or they might want to play. The babysitter must judge the situation carefully.

A good babysitter is hard to find. Many children do not like their baby-sitters. Why? Because the babysitter does not like children, or because the parents did not choose the babysitter carefully.

Answer the questions.

1. What does a good babysitter have to be?

2. Why do young people babysit?

3. Why is babysitting difficult?

4. What might happen to a child?

5. Who must the babysitter call in an emergency?

6. How do children test a new babysitter?

7. Why do many children not like their babysitters?

8. Do you babysit? Why?

THINK

How can you make a fire?
What can fire do?
What must you learn about fire?

phone [ow]

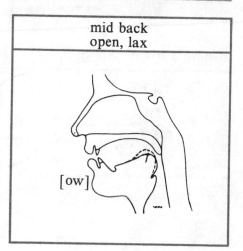

mid back
open, lax

[ow]

go	over	nose
know	radio	told
toe	open	coat
window	joke	snow
road ·	alone	soda
broke	Toronto	drove

Joseph had to go to Toronto. It was cold, and there was snow on the road.
He drove alone and listened to the radio.

Did you notice those roses under the window?
Yes. They're growing very well.
I'm going to write a poem about them.

UNIT 11

Inviting a friend skiing.

Bill:

Hello, Mrs. Martin. Is Edward home?

Mrs. Martin:

Yes, he is. Edward, Bill would like to see you.

Edward:

Hi, Bill. How are you?

Bill:

Fine. We're going skiing. Can you come with us?

Edward:

I'd like to go, but I should finish

my homework first.

Bill:

Could you go this afternoon?

Edward:

Yes, that would be fine.

Bill:

O.K. I'll see you at one o'clock.

ADAPTATION

Construct new sentences like the models using the cues.

Mrs. Martin. Edward?

Bill.

Hello, Mrs. Martin. Is Edward home?

Yes, he is. Edward, Bill would like to see you.

Mr. Coleman. Barbara?

_____ . _____ ?

Elizabeth.

_____ . _____ .

Mrs. Gordon. Charles?

_____ . _____ ?

Victor.

_____ . _____ .

Mr. Johnson. Linda?

_____ . _____ ?

Janet.

_____ . _____ .

Mrs. Wilson. Paul?   _____ . _____?

Robert.   _____ . _____.

2

We, skiing.   **We're going skiing.**

come, us?   **Can you come with us?**

I, swimming.   _____ .

come, me?   _____ ?

They, dancing.   _____ .

go, them?   _____ ?

He, fishing.   _____ .

go, him?   _____ ?

She, shopping.   _____ .

go, her?   _____ ?

184

3

finish my homework.

I'd like to go, but I should finish my homework first.

study history.

_____ .

make a cake.

_____ .

paint my bedroom.

_____ .

wash my clothes.

_____ .

4

go, this afternoon?

Could you go this afternoon?

fine.

Yes, that would be fine.

come, tonight?

_____ ?

great.

_____ .

be there, tomorrow?

_____ ?

terrific.

_____ .

be there, at two?

_____ ?

O.K.

_____ .

185

The modal auxiliary WOULD: *Bill would like to see you*.

Notice the meaning and use of WOULD:

— What would you do?
— I would buy the tickets today.

— Would you buy four tickets?
— No, I wouldn't. I'd buy two.

Use WOULD for the conditional future. The contraction of WOULD is *'D: I'd buy the tickets today*. The negative contraction is WOULDN'T.

PRACTICE

Change the following sentences using *would* and the cues. Use the affirmative or the negative as appropriate.

He is a good man. / hurt.
→ He would not hurt you.

She is a good woman. / help.
→ She would help you.

It is a good horse. / kick.
⟶ **It would not kick you.**

It is a good dog. / bite.

He is a good teacher. / teach.

She is an intelligent girl. / tell.

They are nice people. / welcome.

Frank is a good friend. / leave.

She is a good sister. / excuse.

It is a dangerous animal. / kill.

STUDY 2

The modal auxiliary COULD: *Could you go this afternoon?*

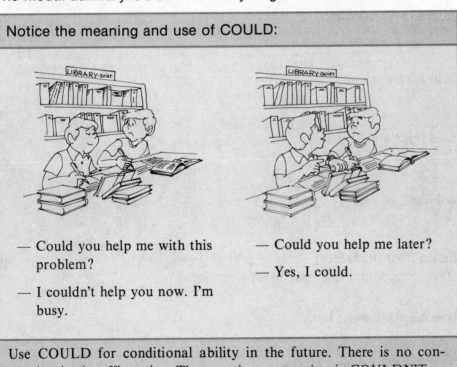

Notice the meaning and use of COULD:

— Could you help me with this problem?

— I couldn't help you now. I'm busy.

— Could you help me later?

— Yes, I could.

Use COULD for conditional ability in the future. There is no contraction in the affirmative. The negative contraction is COULDN'T.

Ask and answer the questions using *could* and the cues.

help me? busy.

Could you help me?
Yes, I could, but I'm busy now.

read this? tired.

Could you read this?
Yes, I could, but I'm tired now.

memorize this? resting.

repeat that? thinking.

help her? working.

hold this? busy.

call him? going out.

fix the TV? tired.

translate this? busy.

read this? resting.

The modal auxiliary SHOULD: *I should finish my homework first*.

Notice the meaning and use of SHOULD:

— Should he go to school?
— No. He should stay home.

— What should he do?
— He should stay in bed. He shouldn't get up.

Use SHOULD for advice and recommendations. SHOULD is not as strong as MUST. MUST means obligation. There is no contraction in the affirmative. The negative contraction is SHOULDN'T.

PRACTICE

1 Change each sentence following the models, using *should* and the cues.

John has a test tomorrow. / study tonight.
→ **He should study tonight.**

Her TV doesn't work. / fix it.
→ **She should fix it.**

Sylvia is sick. / see a doctor.

Bill is tired. / go to bed early.

James is thirsty. / drink some orange juice.

Ann doesn't understand the exercise. / talk to the teacher.

Robert doesn't know the answer. / look in the dictionary.

Paul works very hard. / study yoga.

Mary didn't hear the questions. / listen carefully.

Carl is hungry. / eat lunch now. .

2 Change each sentence following the models, using *must* and the cues.

You are sick. / stay in bed.
→ You must stay in bed.

Vincent has a test tomorrow. / study tonight.
→ He must study tonight.

Charles doesn't know the dialogue. / memorize it.

His radio doesn't work. / fix it.

Joseph is very sick. / go to the hospital.

I have to go to work at seven o'clock. / get up early.

You're going to Japan. / learn Japanese.

Alice didn't read the book. / go to the library.

Pierre is going to the United States. / learn English.

Frank doesn't know the telephone number. / ask Larry.

Make as many sentences as you can about the following statements. Use *should, must, could, will,* and *might*.

Mary has an exam, but she is tired.
→ **She should rest. / She should study. / She must prepare. etc.**

Alice wants to go to the football game, but her father said no.
→ **She can't go to the game. / She must stay home. etc.**

Robert's car doesn't work.

Alice is very sick.

I need a new coat.

George is buying a new motorcycle.

My father can't eat meat.

Paul wants to take a vacation.

SPEAK

1 John and His Father

J.: Could we go fishing
     tomorrow, Dad?

F.: I can't, John. I'm busy tomorrow.
     You should ask Daniel to go with you.

J.: I would ask him, but he doesn't like to fish.

F.: All right, John. We'll try to go tomorrow.

J.: That's great. Thanks!

2 Patricia and Christine

C.: Hello! May I speak to Patricia, please?

P.: This is Patricia. Who is this?

C.: Oh, hello, Patricia. This is Christine. Could you give me Victor's phone number? I have to call him.

P.: I don't have his phone number. You should call Sylvia. She knows it.

C.: All right. I'll do that. I'll call you later.

P.: O.K. Good-bye Christine.

C.: Good-bye.

READ

What should we do to stay healthy? First, we should exercise often. Exercise is good for the body.

The Gordon family tries to exercise every day. Mr. Gordon cannot exercise in the morning because he must be at the office at exactly seven o'clock. But he jogs every evening. He could stay home and read the newspaper, but he prefers to run. His son James likes to exercise too. He walks to school every day, and after school he plays hockey with his friends. Mrs. Gordon cannot walk to work. She must go by bus because their house is far from her office. But she walks to the store on Monday, Wednesday and Friday, and she goes swimming twice a week.

A good diet is important for the body too. Every day the Gordons have vegetables and meat or fish for dinner. Sometimes they have fresh fruit for dessert. James prefers to eat ice cream and cookies, but his father always tells him: "An apple a day keeps the doctor away."

Answer the questions.

1. Who tries to exercise every day?

2. What does Mr. Gordon do every evening?

3. Could he stay home and read the newspaper?

4. Can he exercise in the morning? Why?

5. What does James do in the morning?

6. Can Mrs. Gordon walk to work?

7. How must she go to the office?

8. What does the family eat for dinner?

9. What should we do to stay healthy?

Prepare a brief discussion on what people should do to stay healthy. Use the pictures as cues and the words *could, should, must*.

foot [u]	high back, close, tense
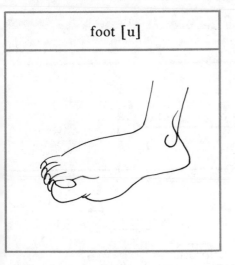	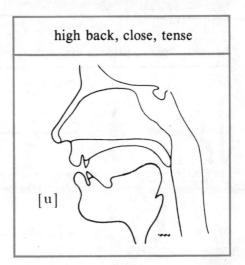
	[u]

foot	would
put	woman
could	look
cookies	should
book	good

Mrs. Woods is a very good cook. You would like her cookies. They look good and taste good. I would make some cookies but I can't find her cookbook. Should I ask her for it?

195

UNIT 12

Arriving home after a shopping trip.

Barbara:

What did you buy in Montreal?

Mrs. Martin:

I bought two spring coats, one for you

and one for your brother.

Barbara:

Which one is mine?

Mrs. Martin:

The first one is yours. The second one is his.

Barbara:

Did you bring me any gloves?

Mrs. Martin:

Yes. I brought you some gloves and I brought

your brother a sweater.

Barbara:

Thank you!

Construct new sentences like the models using the cues.

in Montreal?

two spring coats.

What did you buy in Montreal?

I bought two spring coats.

in Quebec City?

a raincoat.

_____ ?

_____ .

in Madrid?

some shoes.

_____ ?

_____ .

in Paris?

some ties.

_____ ?

_____ .

197

in Rome?

some gloves.

_____ ?

_____ .

2

mine?

first.

Which one is mine?

The first one is yours.

hers?

second.

_____ ?

_____ .

ours?

third.

_____ ?

_____ .

theirs?

fourth.

_____ ?

_____ .

his?

fifth.

_____ ?

_____ .

3

gloves?

sweater.

Did you bring me any gloves?

Yes. I brought you some gloves and I brought your brother a sweater.

shoes?

coat.

_____ ?

_____ . _____ .

socks?

hat.

_____ ?

_____ . _____ .

dresses?

shirt.

_____ ?

_____ . _____ .

boots?

raincoat.

_____ ?

_____ . _____ .

Possessive pronouns: *Which one is mine?*

Notice the use of MINE, YOURS, OURS, THEIRS, HIS, HERS:

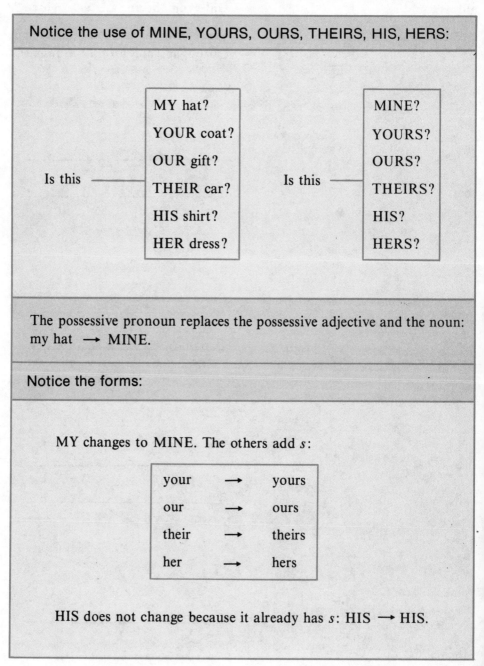

Is this ———

MY hat?

YOUR coat?

OUR gift?

THEIR car?

HIS shirt?

HER dress?

Is this ———

MINE?

YOURS?

OURS?

THEIRS?

HIS?

HERS?

The possessive pronoun replaces the possessive adjective and the noun:
my hat → MINE.

Notice the forms:

MY changes to MINE. The others add *s*:

your	→	yours
our	→	ours
their	→	theirs
her	→	hers

HIS does not change because it already has *s*: HIS → HIS.

1 Repeat the first sentence and add a second one, using the appropriate possessive pronoun.

This is not John's hat.
→ **This is not John's hat. He wants his.**

These are not Helen's gloves.
→ **These are not Helen's gloves. She wants hers.**

These are not Paul's boots.

This is not her blouse.

These are not the boys' sweaters.

This is not Mary's winter coat.

This is not Bill's raincoat.

These are not Tom's shoes.

2 Answer the questions according to the pictures.

Is this your book?
→ **Yes, it's mine.**

Is this Helen's pencil?
→ **No, it's not hers.**

Are these John's glasses?

Is this their car?

Are these Philip's scissors?

Is this his pen?

201

Is this David's tie?

Are these his shoes?

STUDY 2

Ordinal numbers: *first, second, third*,...

Notice the endings of the ordinals:

CARDINALS	ORDINALS	
one	first	(1st)
two	second	(2nd)
three	third	(3rd)
twenty-one	twenty-first	(21st)
twenty-two	twenty-second	(22nd)
twenty-three	twenty-third	(23rd)
thirty-one	thirty-first	(31st)
etc.		

The first three ordinals and the other numbers in which they appear are irregular.

Add *-th* to form other ordinals (*indicates a spelling change):

four	fourth	(4th)
five	*fi<u>f</u>th	(5th)
six	sixth	(6th)
seven	seventh	(7th)
eight	*eig<u>h</u>th	(8th
nine	*nin<u>t</u>h	(9th)
ten	tenth	(10th)
eleven	eleventh	(11th)
twelve	*twel<u>f</u>th	(12th)
thirteen	thirteenth	(13th)
twenty	*twent<u>ie</u>th	(20th)

1 Read the sentences aloud.

This is the first time.

The second will be tomorrow.

The third will be next week.

The first month of the year is January.

The twelfth month is December.

The last day of the year is December 31st.

2 Answer the questions using the ordinals.

What month of the year is May?
→ The fifth month.

What day of the month is Christmas?
→ The twenty-fifth.

What month is November?

What day of the year is New Year's Day?

What month is your birthday?

What day of the month is your birthday?

Use of ANY/SOME: *Did you bring me any gloves?*

Notice the use of ANY and SOME:

Do you have — ANY / SOME — envelopes?

Yes, I have SOME.

No, I don't have ANY.

Use either ANY or SOME in a question. Use ANY when you answer a question in the negative.

ANY means "at least one" or "at least a little":
Do you have any brothers? Do you have any paper?

SOME means "more than one" or "more than a little":
Do you have some magazines? Do you have some chocolate?

1 Answer the questions according to the pictures. Use *some* or *any*.
Rosemary and Alice are making a cake.

a.

b.

c.

d.

e.

f.

g.

h.

a. **Do they have any sugar?**
→ **Yes, they have some.**

b. **Does Rosemary want some salt?**
→ **No, she doesn't want any.**

c. Do they have any flour?

d. Do they have some eggs?

e. Does Rosemary want some bananas?

f. Does Alice want some apples?

g. Do they have any milk?

h. Do you want some cake?

2 Read the sentences aloud. Use *some* or *any*.

I have **some** salt, but I don't have **any** sugar.

He didn't buy ___*any*___ books, but he bought ___*some*___ records.

They did not sell ___*any*___ newspapers, but they sold ___*some*___ magazines.

She has ___*some*___ stamps, but she doesn't have ___*any*___ envelopes.

We caught ___*some*___ fish yesterday, but we didn't catch ___*any*___ last Thursday.

He didn't see ___*any*___ children, but he saw ___*some*___ women.

You brought ___*some*___ oranges, but you didn't bring ___*any*___ bananas.

I didn't eat ___*any*___ cookies today, but I ate ___*some*___ last night.

STUDY 4

Irregular past in [ɔ] : *saw, thought*.

Learn or review these irregular past forms:		
The past of	SEE	is SAW.
	TEACH	TAUGHT.
	CATCH	CAUGHT.
	BUY	BROUGHT.
	BRING	BROUGHT.
	THINK	THOUGHT.
Pronounce these irregular past forms with [ɔ].		

Answer with *yes*. Use the pictures as cues.

Did you buy any books?
→ **Yes, I bought two.**

Did he bring some eggs?
→ **Yes, he brought a dozen.**

Did you catch some fish?

Did John bring any money?

Did she see any friends?

 Pat Paul

Did he teach English?

Did he bring you something?

1 Helen and Mary

H.: What's your favorite food?

M.: I love fried chicken. That's my first choice.
    What's yours?

H.: Mine is fish. I like it with onions and potatoes.
    Don't you like fish?

M.: Yes. Fish is my second choice.

2 James and Nancy

N.: What did you bring me?

J.: I brought you two things — a record and a bottle
    of wine. Which one do you want first?

N.: The wine, please. I'll play the record later.

3 | Kenneth and Gloria

G.: What's today?

K.: Today is the first day of the month.

G.: Oh, no! Yesterday was my cousin's birthday, and I forgot to call her.

K.: What are you going to do?

G.: I'll send her a card.

READ

Many people like their own national food and a variety of foreign ones. You can find international restaurants in any large city and in many small cities. You can find Oriental and European restaurants — Spanish, French, Chinese, and Japanese — in Montreal, Toronto, Vancouver, and in many other cities in Canada. In the capital of any country you can find almost any type of food.

American hamburgers and hot dogs are popular in Canada and in Europe. And French pastries are luxury foods in Montreal and New York. In almost every country you will find rice, potatoes, eggs, bread, soup, meat, vegetables, milk, fruit, and other basic foods. But in each country people cook them differently.

People also prefer different things to drink. England is famous for its tea and France is famous for its wine. German beer is now completely international.

Answer the questions.

1. Are your favorite foods national or international?

2. What are your favorite foods?

3. What is your favorite restaurant?

4. What would be your first, second, and third choices in a restaurant?

5. What are some luxury foods in Canada?

6. What kind of potatoes do you like?

7. Do you like to try new foods?

8. What do you prefer to drink?

9. What kinds of foods do you find in almost every country?

THINK

John and Carol are thinking about their favorite foods. Answer the questions using the pictures as cues.

1. What are John's favorite foods?

2. What does Carol like to eat?

3. What might they eat for dinner?

4. What does John like for breakfast?

5. What might Carol have for breakfast?

6. Who is on a diet?

7. What might they have for lunch?

8. When would John eat cake?

9. Would Carol eat ice cream? Why?

10. Who would eat a hamburger?

11. What are your favorite foods?

PRONOUNCE

Paul [ɔ].	low, back, open
	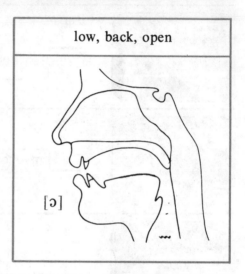

August	often	bought
fall	long	walk
coffee	office	always
saw	tall	talk

I saw Mr. Dawson yesterday. He was walking with a tall man.

Did you talk to him?

No. I was shopping. I bought a long scarf and some socks.

Why a scarf? It's only August.

Yes, but fall and winter are just around the corner.

211

UNIT 13

Asking for information.

John:

Does anybody in town fix radios?

Mine doesn't work.

David:

Someone must. Try Edison's Radio Shop.

John:

Does anyone know the address?

David:

I don't. No one here does.

John:

Maybe I should look it up in the phone book.

David:

That's a good idea. You can find almost anything

in the phone book.

John:

Thanks. I'll do that.

Construct new sentences like the models using the cues.

1

radios?

Edison's Radio Shop.

Does anybody in town fix radios?

Someone must. Try Edison's Radio Shop.

TV's?

Hill's TV Shop.

_____ ?

_____ . _____ .

cameras?

the Camera Shop.

_____ ?

_____ . _____ .

watches?

the Time Shop.

_____ ?

_____ . _____ .

typewriters?

Mr. Green's store.

_____ ?

_____ . _____ .

213

2

address?   **Does anyone know the address?**

I.   **I don't. No one here does.**

telephone number?   _____ ?

She.   _____ . _____ .

name?   _____ ?

He.   _____ . _____ .

manager?   _____ ?

We.   _____ . _____ .

price?   _____ ?

I.   _____ . _____ .

phone book.

Maybe I should look it up in the phone book.

Yes. You can find almost anything in the phone book.

dictionary.

_____ .

_____ .

newspaper.

_____ .

_____ .

encyclopedia.

_____ .

_____ .

yellow pages.

_____ .

_____ .

Indefinite pronouns combining SOME-, ANY-, EVERY-, NO- with -BODY and -ONE: *Does anybody in town fix radios?*

Notice the combination and use of SOME-, ANY-, EVERY-, NO-, with -BODY, -ONE:

SOMEbody	=	SOMEone
ANYbody	=	ANYone
EVERYbody	=	EVERYone
NObody	=	NO one

SOMEBODY
SOMEONE
> can fix it.

Can
ANYBODY
ANYONE
fix it?

Where is
EVERYBODY?
EVERYONE?

NOBODY
NO ONE
> wanted to stay.

-BODY and -ONE have the same meaning. All of the combinations except NO ONE are one word.

Answer the questions. Use short answers with *everybody, anybody, somebody, nobody, everyone, anyone, someone* or *no one*.

The music was beautiful. Who liked it? /everyone
→ **Everyone did.**

The story was interesting. Who was bored? / no one
→ **No one was.**

The concert is free. Who can attend? / anybody

The story was simple. Who understood it? / everybody

The lesson was difficult. Who liked it? / nobody

The exercise was not long. Who finished it? / everyone

The test is tomorrow. Who should study? / everyone

It's a difficult question. Nobody wants to answer it. Who should answer it? / somebody

English is easy. Who can learn it? / anyone

The board is clean. Who erased it? / someone

Indefinite pronouns combining SOME-, ANY-, EVERY-, NO- with -THING, -WHERE: *You can find almost anything in the phone book.*

> Notice the combination of SOME-, ANY-, EVERY-, NO-, with -THING, -WHERE:

SOMEthing	SOMEwhere
ANYthing	ANYwhere
EVERYthing	EVERYwhere
NOthing	NOwhere

I saw him SOMEWHERE before.

We couldn't find him ANYWHERE.

Why does EVERYTHING happen to me?

There is NOTHING on the table.

When NO- combines with -THING the vowel sound of "o" changes from [ow] to [ə].

> Notice the singular verb form with the use of EVERY-:

All of the people are here.   →   EVERYBODY is here.

All of the things are electric.   →   EVERYTHING is electric.

1 Answer the questions with *nothing, nobody, everywhere* or *somebody*.

a.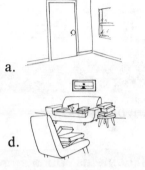

b.

c.

d.

e.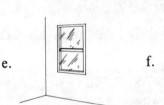

f.

a. **What is on the floor?**
→ **Nothing.**

b. Who is sitting in the chair?

c. Who is talking on the telephone?

d. The books are on the chair, the table and the sofa. Where are the books?

e. Who is standing near the window?

f. What is in the glass?

2 Answer the questions. Use short answers with *everyone, someone, nowhere,* or *no one*.

We all know Bill. Who knows him?

→ **Everyone does.**

She doesn't want to go to school, to church or to the movies. Where does she want to go?

→ **Nowhere.**

It's impossible to talk to him. Who can talk to him?

We left the window open. Now it's closed. Who was here?

The students and the teacher didn't come to school. Who came to school?

John didn't go to the movies. He stayed home. Where did he go?

We all like to watch TV. Who likes to watch TV?

The radio was here. It's not here now. Who took it?

STUDY 3

Combinations with SOME- and ANY-: *Does anybody know the address?*

Notice the use of SOME- and ANY- in statements, questions and in the negative:	
Statements:	I want to see SOMEone.
	I want to go SOMEwhere.
	I want to do SOMEthing.
Questions:	Do you want to see SOMEone/ANYone?
	Do you want to go SOMEwhere/ANYwhere?
	Do you want to do SOMEthing/ANYthing?
Negative:	I don't want to see ANYone.
	I don't want to go ANYwhere.
	I don't want to do ANYthing.

SOME- is usually used in affirmative statements: *He wants something. They're going somewhere.*

SOME- and ANY- are used in questions: *Do you want something? Do you want anything?*

ANY- is used in negative statements: *She doesn't want anything. They're not going anywhere.*

1 Use *everything, something, anybody* or *anything*.

We gave John all the food, boxes, and bottles. We gave him **everything.**

We gave Helen a basket. We have her **something.**

John is rich and happy. He has _____ .

James has no friends. He doesn't like _____ .

All the food is here. We have _____ .

I don't have a coat, a hat or shoes. I don't have _____ .

Mary is sick. She can't visit _____ .

He can't see colors or light. He can't see _____ .

I couldn't see clearly, but I saw _____ .

2 Change to negative sentences using the cues and *either*.

They went nowhere yesterday. / I.
→ **I didn't go anywhere yesterday either.**

We told the secret to no one. / She.
→ **She didn't tell the secret to anyone either.**

Mother cooked nothing today. / Mrs. Hill.
→ **Mrs. Hill didn't cook anything today either.**

The secretary telephoned no one. / Her boss.

The doctor gave the patient nothing. / nurse.

The reporter went nowhere during his vacation. / policeman.

Francis wrote nothing on the paper. / Dale.

The old plane can go nowhere now. / old train.

The lawyer could get no one to help him. / mechanic.

The painter painted nothing for weeks. / Mr. Miller.

She knew no one. / He.

3 Complete the mini-dialogues according to the pictures. Use
something, anything, someone, anyone, somewhere, anywhere.

Do you see anyone in the class?
No. I don't see anyone.

Did Mary go anywhere last night?

_____ . _____ .

_____ ?

Yes. Someone is watching TV.

Does Linda want anything?

_____ . _____ .

Is Paul going to go anywhere on Monday?

_____ . _____ ?

Irregular past in [ey]: *ate, came*.

Learn or review these irregular past forms:

The past of		is	
	EAT		ATE.
	COME		CAME.
	BECOME		BECAME.
	GIVE		GAVE.
	MAKE		MADE.
	PAY		PAID.

Pronounce these irregular past forms with [ey].

PRACTICE

Answer the questions according to the pictures.

Did you eat the cake or the candy?

→ **I ate the cake.**

Did you come to the party with James or Frank?

→ **I came with Frank.**

Frank

Did you give the gift to your sister or to your cousin?

sister

223

Did you become tired or hungry at the soccer game?

Did you make sandwiches or a salad for lunch?

Did you come home alone or with someone?

Did you pay only for the pen or for everything?

Did you eat chicken or fish for dinner?

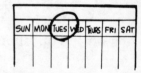

Did you come on Tuesday or on Thursday?

Did you give your paper to Paul or to the teacher?

Did you make this cake or did Bill make it?

Bill

224

1 Patricia and Edith

P.: Did you make a new dress for the party?

E.: Yes. I made one last weekend. Everyone in my family likes it.

P.: Could you make me one too? I can't sew. And clothes are very expensive now.

E.: I'd be happy to do it. I can begin tonight.

2 Mrs. Payne and Mr. Moore

M.: I would like to buy a present for my son. Do you have anything?

P.: Could he use a watch? Everybody needs one.

M.: No. He has one already.

P.: Would he like a radio? That's an excellent gift.

M.: Yes. He could use a radio. I'll take the black one over there.

P.: Robert, do you know Fred Martin?

R.: Yes. Everyone knows him.

P.: Where does he live? I want to tell him something.

R.: He lives on Maple Street. Near the church, I think.

P.: Thanks!

READ

Someone once wrote, "All work and no play makes Jack a dull boy." Work is important, but everyone needs some leisure time. Leisure time means free time. It comes after work. It is the time for anything of interest to you. Some people like to practice sports. Others like to go somewhere. They may go shopping or to the movies.

Many people have hobbies. They make things or collect things. Right now someone is enjoying a hobby somewhere. People collect stamps, coins, rocks, or butterflies. Everyone likes to make something, too. You could make a boat or clothes, a table or a blanket, an animal cage or an apple pie.

People with hobbies are not dull. They are very interesting because they can talk about their leisure activities. Some work and some play will make you interesting too.

Answer the questions.

1. Who needs leisure time?

2. What does it mean?

3. What do some people like to do?

4. What things might someone collect?

5. Could you make a table or a tablecloth?

6. Why aren't people with hobbies dull?

Bill lost his watch. He is talking to Mr. Hill at the "Lost and Found".
Mr. Hill is asking Bill questions. Answer the questions for Bill. Use
everywhere, everybody, etc.

Did anyone find a watch in this store yesterday?
→ Yes. Somebody found a watch here yesterday.

Where did you look for the watch?

Where did you lose it?

Could it be in this department?

Did you try the watch department?

Who did you ask about your watch?

Did the salesmen help you look for your watch?

Did someone tell you to come to the "Lost and Found"?

Did the watch cost a lot of money?

228

pain [ey]	complex vowel; tongue moves from mid-front to high-front position
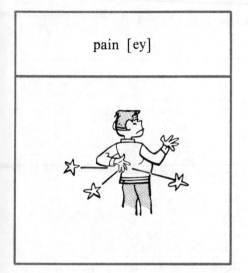	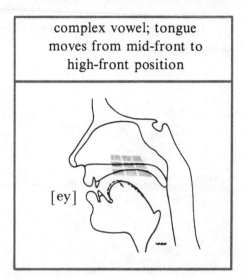[ey]

April	gave	stadium	paper
change	made	James	paintings
plate	rainy	cake	salesman
eighteenth	Dale	radio	mail

Is the mailman late today?

No. There's no mail today. It's Sunday.

But there should be a newspaper.

Yes. It came at 8:30. I gave it to Rachel. She's reading it now.

Why does it always rain in April? We want to play baseball, but every day it rains. There won't be any game at the stadium either. I'll have to stay home.

UNIT 14

Arriving late.

Mother:

Did Howard arrive on time?

Teacher:

No. He was late.

Mother:

How often is he late?

Teacher:

He's always late. He never arrives on time.

Mother:

And how often does he remember to call you?

Teacher:

He seldom remembers. He usually forgets.

Mother:

Does he ever have a good excuse?

Teacher:

Oh, yes. He's usually busy.

ADAPTATION

Construct new sentences like the models using the cues.

1

Howard, arrive on time?　　**Did Howard arrive on time?**

late.　　**No. He was late.**

Susan, get up?　　_____ ?

sick.　　_____ . _____ .

Philip, like the movie?　　_____ ?

bored.　　_____ . _____ .

231

Edith, call?

busy.

_____ ?

_____ . _____ .

Victor, dance?

tired.

_____ ?

_____ . _____ .

he?

always. never.

How often is he late?

He's always late. He never arrives on time.

she?

never. always.

_____ ?

_____ . _____ .

they?

often. seldom.

_____ ?

_____ . _____ .

you?

seldom. usually.

_____ ?

_____ . _____ .

Paul?   ———————————— ?

never. always.   ————— . ————————— .

3

he, call?   **How often does he remember
to call you?**

seldom. usually.   **He seldom remembers. He
usually forgets.**

she, tell?   ———————————— ?

often. seldom.   ————— . ————————— .

Linda, ask?   ———————————— ?

never. always.   ————— . ————————— .

Paul, write?   ———————————— ?

usually. seldom.   ————— . ————————— .

Mary, help?   ———————————— ?

seldom. often.   ————— . ————————— .

4

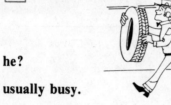

he?

usually busy.

Does he ever have a good excuse?

Oh, yes. He's usually busy.

she?

often tired.

_____ ?

_____ . _____ .

Sarah?

always sick.

_____ ?

_____ . _____ .

Howard?

seldom well.

_____ ?

_____ . _____ .

Barbara?

usually at work.

_____ ?

_____ . _____ .

234

Position of adverbs of frequency: *He's always late. He never arrives on time.*

Notice the position of ALWAYS, USUALLY, OFTEN, SELDOM, NEVER:

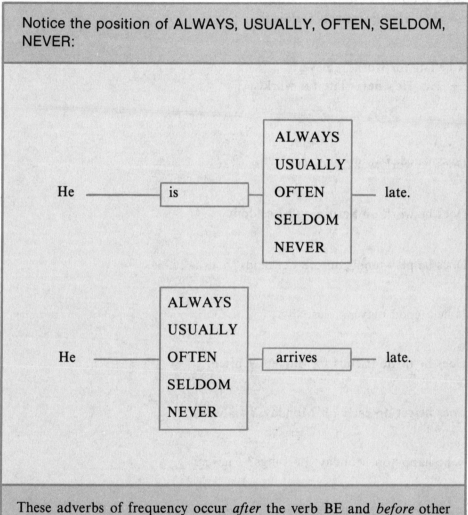

These adverbs of frequency occur *after* the verb BE and *before* other verbs. When the sentence has a modal auxiliary, they occur *after* the modal auxiliary and *before* the main verb:

I will ALWAYS remember you.
I will NEVER forget you.

Answer with *yes* or *no* using the cue words.

Does John act seriously? / always.
→ **Yes. He always acts seriously.**

Is he late for work? / never.
→ **No. He's never late for work.**

Does he work well? / always. *yes*

Does he work on Saturdays? / seldom.

Does he play tennis on the weekends? / usually.

- Is he a good player? / usually.

⌐ Does he invite friends for dinner? / often.

⌐ Does he get up early on Mondays? / always.

— Is he happy on Monday mornings? / never.

Does he go to bed late at night? / often.

Does his mother prepare breakfast in the morning? / usually.

Does his family watch TV at night? / seldom.

236

Use of EVER and NEVER: *He never arrives on time. Does he ever have a good excuse?*

> Notice the use of EVER and NEVER in questions and statements:
>
> Is he EVER on time?
> → No. He's NEVER on time.
>
> Does he EVER arrive on time?
> → No. He NEVER arrives on time.
>
> Use EVER in questions. Use NEVER in statements.

PRACTICE

Complete the sentences and the questions. Use *ever* or *never*.

Is Susan **ever** on time?
→ No. She's **never** on time.

Does Paul _____ sleep late on weekdays?

No. He _____ sleeps late on weekdays.

He _____ goes to bed late either.

Do Susan and Paul _____ walk to the office?

No. They _____ walk to the office.

Is the bus _____ late?

Yes. It's often late.

Do Susan and Paul _____ go dancing on Mondays?

No. They _____ go dancing on Mondays. They're too tired.

HOW OFTEN, HOW FAST: *How often is he late? How fast does he read?*

Notice the meanings of HOW OFTEN and HOW FAST:

HOW OFTEN is he late?
→ He's always late.

HOW OFTEN do you go shopping?
→ Once a week.

Use HOW OFTEN to ask about the *frequency* of an action.

HOW FAST does he read?
→ He reads very fast.

HOW FAST is the mail?
→ It's usually slow.

Use HOW FAST to ask about the *speed* of an action.

Change to questions with *how fast* or *how often*. Then give a short answer.

Mr. Collins reads the newspaper every day.
→ **How often does Mr. Collins read the newspaper?**
→ **Every day.**

He can read very fast.
→ **How fast can he read?**
→ **Very fast.**

Mr. Collins can read two hundred words a minute.

His son seldom reads.

He reads very slowly.

Mrs. Collins drives to the store every Saturday.

She seldom walks to the store.

Their daughter teaches French every day.

She speaks it very fast.

She goes to France every summer.

239

HOW EARLY/LATE, HOW FAR/NEAR: *How early is it? How far is it?*

Notice the meanings of HOW EARLY/LATE and
HOW FAR/NEAR:

HOW EARLY do you get up in the morning?

→ I usually get up at 7:00.

HOW LATE is the restaurant open?

→ Until midnight.

Use HOW EARLY/HOW LATE to ask about *time*.

HOW FAR do you drive to work?

→ I have to drive ten kilometres.

HOW NEAR is the hospital?

→ Two blocks from here.

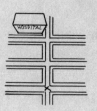

Use HOW FAR/HOW NEAR to ask about *distance*.

1 Change to questions with *how early, how late, how near* or *how far*. Then give a short answer according to the pictures.

Philip gets up early every morning.
→ **How early does he get up?**
→ **At five o'clock.**

He lives far from the office.
→ **How far does he live from the office?**
→ **Twenty kilometres.**

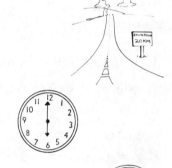

He goes to work early.

Linda usually gets up late.

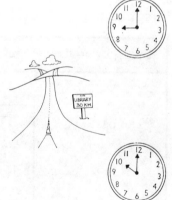

She lives far from the library.

She usually arrives at work late.

Philip and Linda like to go to bed late on Fridays.

They like to get up late on Saturdays.

2 Answer the questions individually.

How often do you go to the movies?

How long is a day?

How far can you throw a baseball?

How well do you speak English?

How interesting is history?

How often do you have a birthday?

How tall are you?

How important is English?

How fast do you walk to school?

How often does Thanksgiving come?

STUDY 5

Irregular past in [ae]: *drank, ran*.

Learn or review these irregular past forms:		
The past of	SIT	is	SAT.
	SING		SANG.
	SWIM		SWAM.
	BEGIN		BEGAN.
	DRINK		DRANK.
	RUN		RAN.

Pronounce these irregular past forms with [ae].

Answer the questions according to the pictures.

What did he drink with his supper?
→ He drank milk.

When did he begin to study?

Where did she sit?

What time did the play begin?

What did he do at the lake yesterday?

What did they do at the talent show?

He was late for school. What did he do?

What did they drink at the picnic?

1 John and Uncle Fred

U.: Happy Birthday, John.

J.: Thank you, Uncle Fred.

U.: Tell me, how often do you walk to school?

J.: Every day. Why do you ask?

U.: I have a surprise for you. Your new bicycle
is in front of the house.

2 Philip and David

P.: David, how old are you?

D.: I'm very old. Can't you see?

P.: You're always joking.

D.: Not always. Sometimes I act seriously.

P.: How often do you do that?

D.: Seldom...but sometimes.

3 Victor and Lawrence

V.: How far can you swim?

L.: About three kilometres.

V.: That's very far! And how fast do you swim?

L.: I usually swim a kilometre in twenty minutes. It's excellent exercise.

V.: How often do you exercise?

L.: Twice a day — once in the morning and again in the evening.

Families usually remember everybody's birthday, and someone in the family will often organize a party. Birthday celebrations are very popular, especially among young people. Good friends always come to the party and they bring gifts. Then everyone plays games. There are always refreshments — usually ice cream, a cake, sandwiches and cookies.

Birthday cakes always have candles. The candles represent the age of the person with one candle for each year. Someone always lights the candles. Then everyone sings "Happy Birthday." The person makes a wish and blows out the candles. The wish is usually a secret.

Adults often celebrate their birthdays too. They usually put one candle on the cake. They seldom want to tell their age. How many candles would you need on your birthday cake?

Answer the questions.

1. Who will often organize a birthday party?

2. Who comes to birthday parties?

3. What do the candles on a cake represent?

4. What do you usually do at birthday parties?

5. How many candles do adults usually have on their cakes?

6. Do adults always celebrate birthdays?

7. Can you sing "Happy Birthday" in English?

8. When is your birthday?

9. Are you going to have a party?

10. Describe your birthday party.

Ask questions with *how often, how fast, how late, how far...*
Answer with *always, sometimes, usually...*

pan [æ]	simple vowel; tongue in low-front position; lips extended to the sides
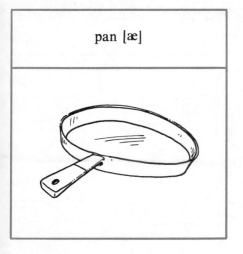	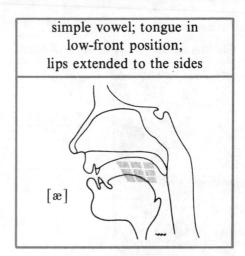

[æ] |

at	bad	fast	magazine
am	last	manager	translator
absent	laugh	sandwich	banana
apple	happy	acrobat	Saturday

I laughed for two hours last night.

What happened?

I saw a movie about a taxi driver. All his passengers forgot things in his taxi. One woman forgot her basket of apples and bananas. A man forgot his magazines. The driver tried to find the passengers, but he couldn't. At last, he drove home with his taxi full of apples, bananas, plants and animals. He was mad, but his wife was happy.

UNIT 15

CONVERSATION

Asking about people and places.

Janet:

Where does Mrs. Martin live?

Mrs. Penfield:

She lives in Granby near the stadium.

Janet:

Is her house on Bell Road?

Mrs. Penfield:

Yes. She lives at 1302 Bell Road.
Do you know her?

Janet:

Yes. I met her at the library last week.

Mrs. Penfield:

I'm going to visit Mrs. Martin on Tuesday.
Shall I say hello for you?

Janet:

Yes, please.

ADAPTATION

Construct new sentences like the models using the cues.

1

Mrs. Martin, live?	**Where does Mrs. Martin live?**
in Granby, stadium.	**She lives in Granby near the stadium.**

Jane, study?

_____ ?

in the library, the post office.

_____ .

Bill, work?

_____ ?

at a restaurant, the school.

_____ .

she, walk?

_____ ?

in the park, the hospital.

_____ .

he, fish?

_____ ?

in the lake, the bridge.

_____ .

2

Bell Road?

1302.

Is her house on Bell Road?

Yes. She lives at 1302 Bell Road.

River Street?

_____ ?

105.

_____ .

St. Joseph Boulevard?

_____ ?

2015.

_____ .

Fifth Avenue?

_____ ?

25.

_____ .

Sherbrooke Street?

_____ ?

5014.

_____ .

3

her?

the library.

Do you know her?

Yes. I met her at the library last week.

John and Charles?

_____ ?

a party.

_____ . _____ .

252

Mr. Martin? _____ ?

the club. _____ . _____ .

me? _____ ?

the school. _____ . _____ .

Keith? _____ ?

the office. _____ . _____ .

4

Mrs. Martin, on Tuesday.

I'm going to visit Mrs. Martin on Tuesday.

say hello for you?

Shall I say hello for you?

Mr. Martin, next week. _____ .

tell him anything? _____ ?

Victor, on Monday. _____ .

give him a message? _____ ?

Janet, this evening.   _____

give her your regards?   _____ ?

Mr. Coleman, tomorrow evening.   _____ .

thank him for you?   _____ ?

STUDY 1

Expressions of place with IN, ON, AT: *She lives in Granby.*

Notice the use of the prepositions IN, ON, AT:

Use IN for cities, towns, provinces, states, countries, continents:

Mary lives	IN Montreal.
Montreal is	IN Quebec.
Quebec is	IN Canada.

Use ON for streets, roads, floors:

She lives	ON Cartier Street.
The museum is	ON Main Street.
Jack works	ON the second floor.

Use AT for specific addresses with numbers:

The museum is	AT 31 Maple Street.
We'll meet her	AT 620 Palm Avenue.
Her office is	AT 444 Forest Road.

Answer with *in, on,* or *at* according to the pictures.

The restaurant should be **at 1242 Main Street.**

Joan lives *in* _____ .

Her home is *in* _____ .

Ethel's Shop was *on* _____ .

London is *in* _____ .

John lives *on* _____ .

We saw Victor *at* _____ .

255

He used to live _on_ _____ .

The accident was _on_ _____ .

STUDY 2

Expressions of time with IN, ON, AT: *I'm going to visit Mrs. Martin on Tuesday.*

Notice the use of the prepositions IN, ON, AT:

Use IN for months, seasons, years, centuries:

Christmas is	IN December.
It rains	IN the spring.
I was born	IN 1960.
Jacques Cartier lived	IN the 16th century.

Use ON for specific dates or days:

Shakespeare was born	ON April 23, 1564.
John's birthday will be	ON Tuesday.
The game will be	ON March 29.

Use AT for holiday times and clock time:

Can they visit us	AT Easter?
The plane left	AT 8:45.
Kenneth should arrive	AT noon.

Answer according to the pictures. Use short answers with *in, on,* or *at*.

When does it snow?

→ **In the winter.**

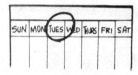

When will Susan have her birthday party?

→ **On Tuesday.**

When is Christmas?

When was Janet born?

When was she born?

What year was she born?

When is Bill going to South America?

What time does Mr. Jones leave work?

When is Susan's vacation?

When does he go home?

STUDY 3

Order of place and time expressions: *I met her at the library last week*.

Notice the order of place and time expressions:

	PLACE	TIME
They were	at home	at noon.
The plane arrived	in Paris	on Tuesday.
He said it	in school	yesterday.
I saw him	on the bus	at 3:30.
We weren't	there	then.
He was reading	in his room	in the evening.

Put the place expression first. Put the time expression second.

1 Construct sentences using the word and picture cues. Use the past tense.

Mary / airport / last night.
→ **Mary worked at the airport last night.**

They / lake / last weekend.
→ **They went fishing at the lake last weekend.**

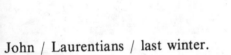

She / park / yesterday.

John / Laurentians / last winter.

They / club / on Saturday night.

Mr. Shaw / courthouse / last month.

Rachel / living room / 8 o'clock.

Jane / restaurant / then.

Frank / garage / last summer.

2 Look at the picture and describe what each person was doing in each room. Use *last night, yesterday* or *at 7 o'clock* in your sentences.

Mr. Clarke was painting a chair in the basement last night.

Roger _____ .

The baby _____ .

Joan _____ .

Mrs. Clarke _____ .

Vivian _____ .

STUDY 4

Irregular past in [e]: *said, left.*

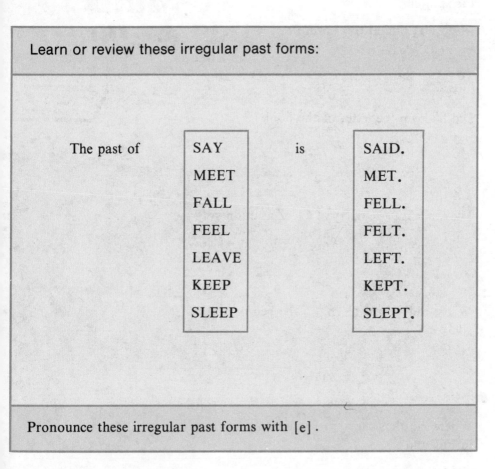

Learn or review these irregular past forms:

The past of		is	
	SAY		SAID.
	MEET		MET.
	FALL		FELL.
	FEEL		FELT.
	LEAVE		LEFT.
	KEEP		KEPT.
	SLEEP		SLEPT.

Pronounce these irregular past forms with [e].

PRACTICE

Answer the questions according to the pictures.

Did you sleep at her house or at a hotel?

→ **I slept at a hotel.**

Did you meet him at the Forum or at the stadium?

→ **I met him at the Forum.**

Did he keep the letter or the book?

Did we leave the party at 11 or at midnight?

Where did Jimmy sleep, on the bed or on the sofa?

Where did they meet, in France or in England?

262

Who did you meet, Linda or John?

What did you say, yes or no?

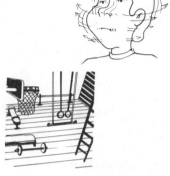

Where did he fall, in the classroom or in the gymnasium?

How did he feel, sick or well?

SPEAK

1 Charles and Keith

C.: When is Thanksgiving?

K.: In October. It's always the second Monday in October.

C.: What does your family do on Thanksgiving?

K.: We usually have a big dinner. We have meat pie with potatoes and sugar pie for dessert. Sometimes we have turkey.

2 Christine and Ann

C.: When will the program start?

A.: At 10 o'clock, I think.

C.: Will it be on Channel 6 or on Channel 12?

A.: I don't know. You could look in the newspaper.

C.: O.K. I will.

3 Read the paragraph and change it to a dialogue between Janet and Susan.

Janet lives in the suburbs of Montreal. She lives far from the city. It takes her about one hour to go home every night. She prefers to live in the suburbs. The houses in the city are small and expensive.

Susan: Where do you live?

Janet: I live...

Continue the dialogue.

READ

New York, Tokyo and Paris are very big and very expensive. Every year thousands of people move to these cities. Many of them are very poor and do not have enough money for food. They cannot find places to live, and they cannot find good jobs. Sometimes their children do not go to school.

Why do people want to move to big cities? Because there are more opportunities there. There are more jobs. There are also good hospitals and good schools. But there are too many people in cities now, and there is not enough food, electricity or gasoline for everyone. Would you invite people for dinner without enough food for them? How could you help people in a

265

school without enough desks or books? How could you help people in a hospital without enough doctors or medicine? People should know about the problems of big cities before they move there.

Are there solutions to these city problems? Nobody knows. In Canada the problems are not too serious. It is not too late to do something. Some people want to limit the population of our cities. Countries limit immigration. We should plan new cities with enough jobs, houses, hospitals, schools and food for everyone.

Answer the questions.

1. Would you like to live in the city or in the country?

2. What big cities do you know?

3. What are the problems of too many people in a big city?

4. What good things can you find in the city?

5. What bad things can you find in the city?

6. Are there solutions to the problems of big cities in Canada?

7. What should people do before they move to the city?

266

Where do you live?

What are the problems of living in the big cities?

What are the good things?

socks [a]	low central, open relaxed, voiced
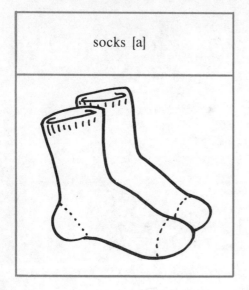	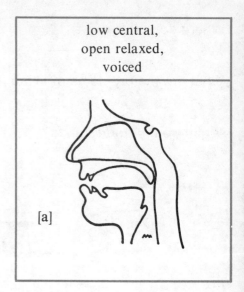 [a]

on	socks	father	hospital
pot	hot	shopping	biology
not	want	concert	astronomy
box	college	problem	Thomas
rocks	doctor	October	o'clock

Dr. Connors is in Ontario on business. He wants to get a gift for his wife, but he has only two dollars in his pocket. He will have to buy it later. But he has another problem. His plane leaves et eight o'clock in the morning. The shops will be closed then.

Donald got up early, but he did not watch the clock. He was late for class and he forgot his biology and geography books. He was late for dinner too. His father was not happy about that. His dinner was not hot; it was cold.

INVENTORY 1

PART I

Choose the correct answer and write the letter in the blank.

Example:

_____a._____ began with John Cabot in 1497?
Canadian history began with John Cabot in 1497.
a. What   b. Where   c. Who   d. When

---

1. Did John Cabot stay in Canada? No, he _____ .
    a. wasn't   b. doesn't   c. weren't   d. didn't

2. Did Cartier _____ to Canada in 1534?
    a. go   b. goes   c. went   d. going

3. _____ title is "The Father of New France".
    a. Champlains   b. Champlain's   c. Champlain   d. Champlains'

4. The French _____ very busy in New France.
    a. was   b. were   c. be   d. am

5. Was Montreal the capital of New France? No, it _____ .
    a. weren't   b. aren't   c. wasn't   d. isn't

6. Canada _____ important to France during the late 1600's.
    a. isn't   b. weren't   c. doesn't   d. wasn't

7. _____ from Quebec usually speak French.
    a. child   b. children's   c. children   d. child's

8. _____ Canadians and Americans like the same sports?
    a. Does   b. Do   c. Are   d. Is

9. Canada _____ a modern country.
   a. is **b.** am **c.** are **d.** be

10. Canada _____ England during World War I.
    a. helps **b.** help **c.** helped **d.** helping

11. _____ is Canada?
    Canada is very beautiful.
    a. How **b.** Who **c.** Where **d.** What

12. _____ do ships from foreign countries come to Canada?
    They come every day.
    a. How **b.** Where **c.** When **d.** Who

13. Are the headquarters of the federal government in Quebec?
    No, _____ not.
    a. he's **b.** they're **c.** it's **d.** we're

14. _____ is opening in Canada now?
    Many new factories are opening.
    a. Who **b.** Where **c.** What **d.** When

15. Does the United States buy paper from _____ Canada?
    a. a **b.** an **c.** the **d.** —

16. _____ do many Canadians live?
    They live in cities.
    a. How **b.** Where **c.** What **d.** Who

17. Canadians make many machines, and they sell _____ to other countries.
    a. its **b.** them **c.** they **d.** their

18. The paper for _____ books came from Canada.
    a. this **b.** that **c.** these **d.** them

270

19. Guy Lafleur _____ hockey very well.
    a. play   **b.** plays   **c.** playing   **d.** was played

20. _____ many Americans in Canada on weekends?
    a. was   **b.** am   **c.** are   **d.** is

21. Please show the students _____ pictures of old Quebec.
    a. its   **b.** you   **c.** they   **d.** your

22. Do Canadians work hard? Yes, they _____ .
    a. does   **b.** do   **c.** did   **d.** don't

PART II

Check the blank for the correct place in the statement or question of the word given on the left. Notice the question marks.

Example:

is   __ Gaspé __ an __ important fishing center __ ?
       a   b   c   d

---

23. not   Canada __ is __ closing __ its doors to people __ from
              a   b   c   d
    other countries.

24. not   __ Montreal __ is __ in Ontario __ .
           a   b   c   d

25. are   __ Montreal __ and Toronto __ important __ cities?
           a   b   c   d

26. ice   __ hockey __ is __ our __ national sport.
           a   b   c   d

271

27. us   Please ___ read ___ the poem ___ about the Acadians ___ .
                a   **b**   **c**   **d**

28. n't   Canada ___ does ___ make ___ many ___ airplanes.
                  a   **b**   **c**   **d**

29. do   ___ Canadians ___ like ___ hockey games ___ ?
         a   **b**   **c**   **d**

30. me   Give ___ it ___ to ___ now.
             a   **b**   **c**

HUN-HUN

INVENTORY 1

For each incorrect answer, check the appropriate section in the REFRESHER UNIT which is found at the beginning of Workbook 2.

	Answer	Refresher Unit Section
1.	d	VIII
2.	a	V
3.	b	XXI
4.	b	X
5.	c	XII
6.	d	X
7.	c	XX
8.	b	IV
9.	a	IX
10.	c	VI
11.	a	XVI
12.	c	XIV
13.	b	XII
14.	c	XV
15.	d	I
16.	b	XIV
17.	b	XVII
18.	c	XIX
19.	b	II
20.	c	XI
21.	d	XXII
22.	b	VII
23.	b	XIII
24.	c	IX
25.	a	XI
26.	a	XXIII
27.	b	XVIII
28.	b	III
29.	a	IV
30.	c	XVIII

INDEX